T0156801

War Drums in the Distance

Special moments in a three year quest for hockey's Holy Grail.

RICHARD (BOOM BOOM) LINDBLOOM

iUniverse, Inc.
New York   Bloomington

iUniverse books may be ordered through booksellers or by contacting:

iUniverse
1663 Liberty Drive
Bloomington, IN 47403
www.iuniverse.com
1-800-Authors (1-800-288-4677)

Because of the dynamic nature of the Internet, any Web addresses or links contained in this book may have changed since publication and may no longer be valid. The views expressed in this work are solely those of the author and do not necessarily reflect the views of the publisher, and the publisher hereby disclaims any responsibility for them.

ISBN: 978-1-4502-6606-2 (sc)
ISBN: 978-1-4502-6607-9 (ebook)

Printed in the United States of America

iUniverse rev. date: 10/26/2010

Contents

Preface

Jimmy Buffet wrote a relatively obscure song entitled "If I could just get it on paper." I'm pretty sure he had a parrot head hat on when he penned it! That song perhaps gives a rhyme and a reason to why I've enjoyed jotting down my discombobulated thoughts after Blackhawk games the past three years. The following verses shed a little light on the following moments that I attempt to describe in this book.

Go to bed wake up with a clear head
Recalling what made it a ball
If I could just get it on paper
I might make some sense of it all.

In trying to "make sense of it all," I'm reminded of a proverb by Lao-tzu – "The journey of a thousand miles begins with the first step." In my mind, the journey that culminated with the Blackhawks hoisting the Stanley Cup on June 9, 2010, began three years ago. That "moment" began when I gazed upon the Hawk rookies, Toews and Kane, At first glance it was obvious we had something very special brewing in Chicago. Not that two players can automatically secure your name on the Cup; far from it. However it was quite apparent the fortunes of Blackhawk hockey were about to take a turn for the better.

Talk about the fast track to success! The following pieces are glimpses into the incredible journey that began in the 07/08 season. You won't find any technical information on hockey, (other than, "hit em, kill em, shoot, you stink ref!), just some stories along the way on that incredible three year ride. You'll find I'm giving over to hyperbole – but also discover the musings of a lifelong fan who follows this game and team with his heart. So, step into the passionate world of Blackhawk hockey with me. Although the names and faces have changed throughout the decades, and even the last three years, this is a story about those warriors who took to heart Denis Savard's famous admonition, "**COMMIT TO THE INDIAN.**"

In the first article I wrote I finished by saying, "what a moment it would be to see the Cup hoisted to the 300 section." As we prepare for the home opener on Oct. 9th, indeed, what a moment it will be when the banner is placed in the rafters of that Madhouse on Madison. Something tells me they'll be a few tears shed as the banner makes its ascent. If it's possible, Jim Cornelison just might take that old Star Spangled Banner up a notch or two. Can you say, "Goose bumps?"

I'd like to thank some very special people for making this book possible. First, thanks to Sam Fels who has occasionally included my 'in depth analysis' of Blackhawk hockey in the true fans program, The Committed Indian. Do not enter the United Center without it. A bit on the irreverent, R-rated side, the boys at Second City Hockey know this game and the nozzles that play it. Secondly, my knowledge of the game has increased exponentially by reading "thethirdmanin.com," the insightful website of Chris Block. I have never failed to read one of his columns that I didn't learn about some aspect of this game. Although I must say it irritated me when he wouldn't blame the refs for some of the Hawks losses – Blasphemy!

My numerous e-mails and on site discussions with RoseLee and Earl Deutsch, who have followed the Hawks since the early 1950's, have been an absolute delight. I'd guess you might say Roselee and I have become hockey pen pals. (Actually e-mail pals – but old habits die hard.) So many times RoseLee would write me back after a game – almost always eliciting a lengthy response from me. Many of those responses unleashed another article tucked away in the recesses of my fragmented mind. She graciously allowed me to use her incredible painting of Maggy for the cover of this book, a painting that in my opinion captures the soul of Blackhawk hockey.

A big thanks to Arla and Don Blocker for the front row seats at their house for "Chicago-Blackhawk-Hockey."

Most importantly, thanks to my wife Nathalie and our children, Taylor and Greg, for adding so much to my life. Little did I know what I was getting into 19 years ago when I said "I do." You've all added so many stories to my life, stories that somehow help to make sense of it all. As was so poignantly pointed out in the song by Andrew Lloyd Weber, love, indeed, changes everything.

Lastly, I'd like to dedicate this book to my mom, Margaret Lindbloom. Winning the Stanley Cup pales in comparison to trying to raise nine children. Despite having a thousand and one other things to do, she always found time to read stories to us. All nine "bloomie's" ensconced around her as she read us a book, remains one of my favorite childhood memories. My love of writing most likely could be traced back to those "special" moments.

Covered by the blood,

Richie (Boom Boom) Lindbloom

12/27/07

War drums in the distance

Special moments; they can't be bought, planned or manufactured. They just happen, spontaneously, with little or no advance warning. We've all had them, and savor them, wishing that life could always be so. One of those moments occurred last Sunday, Dec. 23, 2007 at the United Center. It started with a bone chilling half hour wait in line at the walkup ticket window. As I stood in line, being buffeted by a fierce north westerly wind I could only lament; apparently, the cats out of the bag on this incredibly talented team.

Before going any further, that moment on Dec. 23rd brings to mind three other special moments that have occurred over my 45 years of following those warriors who are fortunate enough to bear the Indian Head on their chests. They include a frigid night In January 1965, watching a special rookie make his debut in a preseason game in 1980 and finally watching the Hawks dynamic duo for the first time this year. (I won't even mention all those moments when I saw Tony "O" standing on his head in the crease, with everything but the kitchen sink being tossed at him.)

The "first moment" occurred when I was 12 years old. If there was 1" of ice on any of the area ponds or rinks, we'd be testing it to see if it would support our weight. Saturday nights were spent in front of a TV watching the Black Hawks at my grandma's house, listening to the incomparable voice of Lloyd Petit while munching on the gooiest candy popcorn known to man. (My Irish grandma loved watching the fights.) Sunday nights our ears were glued to the radio. Alas, coming from a family of 9 kids, there was no way we could afford the high priced $2 tickets for the second balcony in the old barn. The other side of the coin was there were no tickets to buy, every game being a sell out back then.

Miraculously, my dad somehow obtained 5 tickets to a game on a weeknight at the last moment. When we came home from school that day, my mom gave us the news; we were going to see our hero's live for the first time! No sporting event will ever come close to the experience of seeing Hull, Mikita, Nesterenko, Hall, Pilotte, "Moose" Vasko et al. live. The Hawks were butting heads with the Davy Keon and Johnny Bower led Maple Leafs that night and eked out a narrow victory.

After we had trekked up the 2000 stairs to get to the second balcony, I peered over the last row of seats. My eyes were transfixed at my first sight of the rink, at the red and blue clad players warming up. I believe our seats were in the second to last row in the Southwest corner of the Stadium. I've never had a better seat. Believe me when I tell you I spent most of the evening on the edge of it. That night, the Indian Head became firmly implanted in my heart.

On the way home I bet my mom $10 that I would one day be playing in the NHL. Theoretically I still could make the team, so I haven't paid up yet. However at 54 years of age, I do realize time is running out. As we drove by the old Magi-Kist sign on the Dan Ryan, I felt like I had just won the lottery.

The "second moment" occurred in the fall of 1980 when my brother and I went to a preseason game to check out the Hawks new prospects. The team the prior year was led offensively by Reggie Kerr. It also featured one of the best pugilists to ever don the Indian Head, Terry Ruskowski. One of the players we came to check out was a diminutive center who the Hawks obtained largely by default. (Remember, the Hawks probably would have taken Doug Wickenheiser had he not been selected by Montreal first.) After the Habs picked Wickenheiser, nearly setting off riots in Quebec, we had to settle for a scrappy little speedster named Savard.

As my brother and I watched #18 with considerable interest, "the moment" happened. Savard was flying up the left wing along the benches with a defenseman lining him up for an all expense paid trip into row 10 of section 103. Savard deked to the inside, went wide and then put on the afterburners. He went in all alone on the goalie, untouched by the first of many NHL defensemen who would struggle to stop him over his career. I don't believe he scored on the play; however, all I could do was smile and say, "John, did you see that!" It was at that moment we both new we had something special in this diminutive rookie.

In a lesser moment, Savard treated us to one of the funniest happenstances I've ever seen at a hockey game. Rockem Sockem Robot, Ty Domi of the Maple leafs, did something to aggravate Savard as the two went to their respective benches for a line change. Savard, in one of his less brilliant moments, gave Domi a little jab with his stick as they crossed paths. Domi just stood in front of the Hawk bench smiling as if to say, "Dennis, you didn't really mean to do that, did you?" It was if he wanted Dennis to apologize to him so he wouldn't have to kill him next shift. I recall Savard avoided making eye contact as he warily sat on the bench between two of the biggest Hawks he could find.

The 3rd moment was my first look at Toews and Kane. That same old, "John, did you see that," feeling consumed me. Toews's goal against the Avalanche brought the crowd to their feet for over a minute. I personally have never celebrated a goal as long as I did that one. Kane, who I read was the number one draft pick only do to a weak draft, was electrifying. Can you say, "eyes in the back of your head" or "a feather touch on passes" or a "nose for scoring." Good Lord, we can only pray for more weak drafts if Kaner is the result. He's a tricky little devil. (Little did I know how true this description of Kane would turn out!)

Well, those moments bring me full circle to the moment I witnessed on Sunday, the 23rd vs. the Oilers. The Hawks were coming back after a scintillating overtime victory over Ottawa, the top team in the Eastern Conference, the night before. Prior to this time you had no problem walking up to a ticket window and getting a cheap seat within 5 minutes. Not this night though, it's as if a "Great Awakening" occurred. The ticket lines were over 30 people deep. By the time we got to the window, only $30 tickets were left and the game was 8 minutes old. "The Moment" proved to be worth the wait and the extra $15 we had to pay!

The game was vigorously contested, finding the Hawks clinging to a precarious one goal lead before over 22,000 finger nail biting fans for most of the 3rd period. I breathed a sigh of relief every time the Lang/Ruutu/Kontiola line took the ice. They dominated the puck and Ruutu delivered an "Atomic" hit that brought 22,000 blood thirsty fans to their feet, even while it knocked an Oiler defenseman off his. I immediately looked for the nearest orange arm band to go up, even though from a Hawk fans perspective it appeared to be a perfectly legal collision.

Adam (I think I'll play the last minute without a stick) Burrish was another young Hawk that caught my eye that night. He brought a lot of frenetic energy to the frozen pond. It appeared he spent most of the evening flying around the ice looking for someone to go "Postal" on. Keep an eye on this erstwhile Badger. You certainly will not find him or Ruutu leading any sensitivity seminars in the near future.

At any rate, after the Hawks successfully staved off a furious 6 on 4 assault by the Oilers for the last 90 seconds, "The Moment" happened. Martin LaPointe started clapping his hands while looking up to us second cousins in the 300 level. We fans in the nose bleeds went wild. In what turned out to be one huge group hug, the fans in the U.C. fell in love with this team at that moment. Yet, an even bigger "Moment" was to come.

After the 3 stars were announced, (Ruutu should have been one of them), the Hawks one by one returned to the ice, applauded and waved to their fans. I told my daughter that in 40 years of watching Chicago Sport's, I've never witnessed anything quite like that moment. It proved to be the moment "The Indian Head" was firmly implanted in Taylor's heart. She even talked my wife into letting us go to the next game against the Predators, our 3rd game in a row.

After we came home from the Predator game, I couldn't talk very well. I'm afraid my daughter is seeing a side of me I'm not sure I want her to see. As we recapped the game for my wife, she asked me what was wrong with my voice. Taylor quickly interjected, "Dad was yelling at the refs a lot." As if they could here me in sec. 312 row 16!

In conclusion, as I gazed at the Indian Head this week, I noticed something that never struck me before. The brave appears to be smiling. I've been smiling since the Toews goal last year against the Avalanche. While the politically correct crowd continues to get worked up about team mascots, there is nothing derogatory about the Indian Head that adorns center ice. It appears that many of the young Hawks are realizing what a privilege it is to be wearing the Hawks storied jersey. Any tribe would be glad to have the braves that are skating for the Hawks this year.

In fact, if you listen closely, you can hear the muffled sounds of "war drums in the distance," rising all the way to the rafters. Now this is just crazy talk, but what a "moment" it would be to see the Stanley Cup hoisted to the 300 section. Obviously I'm delusional, but the drums are getting louder.

12/26/07

You might be a Blackhawk fan if...

- you cheered when Tom Lysiak tripped the linesman.
- you actually saw a game when the goalies wore no masks.
- you would go into a corner to chase down a loose puck with Chuck Norris, even though you realized it meant instant death by a roundhouse kick to the head.
- the first two words you ever spoke were, "Detroit sucks."
- the second two words were, "Dino Sucks."
- you parked your car 3 blocks away and paid some neighborhood kid $2 to "watch" your car, more than a little concerned your hubcaps would be missing when you returned.
- you remember exactly where you were the night Bobby Hull scored his 50th.
- you saw Stan Mikita, standing on the on the penalty bench using his stick as a baton. He was acting like a symphony conductor at the Forum when the Montreal fans were booing him for some sort of bad behavior. (Probably for carving a Hab up with his wickedly curved stick.) While it did not rival Beethoven's fifth, even the Montreal fans started laughing at his antics.
- you head home after the last game of the season and your 14 year old daughter says, "What am I going to do for the next 4 months?"
- your preseason regimen includes watching "Miracle" 10 times and "Slapshot" at least thrice, in the month of September.
- you sang "Wooly Bully" at the top of your lungs when the hard working Ted Bulley would score or try to fuse an opponents face and the Plexiglas into one.
- you realize hard checks in the corner lead to goals.
- you'd always chuckle when the organist would play "Three blind mice," when the referee and two linesmen would take the ice. (They only had one ref way back when.)
- you wondered how "One" referee could keep an eye on 12 players and the puck at the same time.
- even though you realized he was a hack, you admired Billy Smith's ability to try and castrate an opponent parked outside his crease, while keeping a wary eye on the referee at the same time to avoid detection.
- you recall when the fans made the noise at the "Old Barn," not an obnoxious, excessively loud PA system that is trying to recreate a moment it is incapable of. Hawk games are not Bull games, knock it off.

- you realized early in the preseason that the Hawks were loaded for bear this year. Also that Versteeg and Bolland are just a notch below Toews and Kane.
- you realize Byfuglien = Buff-lin.
- your last prayer before bedtime is that Martin's shoulder continues to stay in its socket.
- the carol, "Little Drummer Boy" reminds you of the 5 or 6 drummers who used to patrol the balconies at the stadium, trying to energize the fans when lackluster play had just about put the fans to sleep.
- you realize those drummer boys beat the hell out of the electronically manufactured noise that just about shatters your ear drums. Again, knock it off.
- you remember climbing about 12 flights of stairs to reach your seats in the second balcony at the Stadium, sometimes running up them if you got caught in traffic.
- you were one of the 7-8000 inextinguishable fans that sat through the lean years, when the U.C. more closely resembled a morgue. While cold bodies are still present, they're moving a lot faster this year.
- although the conditions prevented you from making it into work, you view severe weather warnings as a challenge, never an impediment, to getting to a Hawk game. Although there were times you wondered if your car would be starting when you left. (mainly talking about 300 section people here.) Most likely the kid you paid $2 to watch your car does not have jumper cables.
- you realize there is just something that is very right about walking into the U.C. when the temperature is below zero.
-you have the Indian Head tattooed somewhere on your body.
- your wife, while looking through the Hawks official program, looks at Sharp and says, "Ooooh, look at this one, he's cute." Immediately your 14 year old daughter says, "mom, you don't pick hockey players because their cute." That's my girl, although it turns out Sharpie is much more than a pretty face.
- you've wanted to physically harm a referee.
- you threw a fedora, not a baseball cap, when someone scored a hat trick.
- you can state the members of the RPM, Scooter and Million Dollar lines.
-you remember Maggie taking karate lessons in the offseason.
- you actually laughed when you first saw Maggie try to use karate in a fight. (If only Chuck Norris could have been his sensei. The problem is, Maggie would have died by a round house kick to the head in training. It would take more than one, the first time someone did not die instantly from a Chuck Norris

roundhouse kick to the head. Obviously, as always the case with Keith's bouts, there would be a copious amount of blood to clean up.)

- you realize Maggie was the epitome of a hockey player. You can't play this game without heart, passion and teammates who got your back.

- you listened to Dennis Savards post game tirade on the way home from last years Bluejacket game.

- you can't understand how the slogan, "Commit to the Indian," is not this teams battle cry.

- you want the trumpets (Ode to the working man) that play before the old film highlights played at your wedding or funeral. Forget about what Dire Straits says about "no trumpet playing band," those horns prepare the fans for battle.

- you like it when a Canadian team comes to town so you also get to hear "Oh Canada - glorious and free..."

- you realize not all the true fans sit in the 300 section. The two friends who sit in row 15 of section 101 have forgotten more about hockey than I know. The older couple (Upper 70's?) that sit in front of them are an inspiration, and I guarantee you that gentleman at least once threw a fedora out onto the ice!

- you think sitting outside at Wrigley Field, despite being a Sox fan, on January 1st, and paying exorbitant prices to do it, is one of the smartest decisions you've ever made. The jury remains out on this issue. However, with a little luck and a lot of hard work, we could be vying for first place that day.

- you watched #24, Doug Wilson, crank one up and let it fly; now that Hawkheads, was a slapper.

- you weren't afraid to show your emotional side, maybe even let your eyes water a little, when # 18 got a prolonged and loud ovation when introduced on Pilotte-Magnusson appreciation night.

- your daughter thinks that part of her home schooling curriculum is attending every Hawk practice.

- deep in your heart you really don't want to see any Blackhawk player win the Lady Bing award.

- Stan Mikita get's a dispensation for winning it because he led the league in penalties the year before.

- you saw Jean Beliveau, Gil Perrault or Jean Ratelle and can admit it was a joy to behold such grace and skill.

- you realize Duncan Keith is the teams MVP. He is a Mikhail Baryshnikov on skates.

one of the best, if not the best, sport's article written all year was Rick Morrissey's article on the Hawks attending Dale Tallon's father's wake.

- you wanted to see Bobby Clarke get his lunch handed to him, although under your breath you wish he were a Hawk. I know I'm nuts, but Colin Fraser reminds of the instigating pest from Philadelphia.
-you think the "Committed Indian" should be required reading for all Hawk fans.
- you're just crazy enough to think the Hawks could end this season with a win!

3/29/09

Agony and Ecstasy

What is it about hockey that keeps us clamoring for more? After two scintillating victories, we were left with no recourse but to the beating of chests, pulling of hair and wailing last Sunday, after being vanquished by the hair pulling Canucks. Emily Dickinson put it so well,

For each ecstatic instance,
we must in anguish pay,
in keen and quivering ratio,
to the ecstasy.

Why is it that I take the loss and humiliation so personally, or celebrate after a game like the Devils as if it was I who scored the winning goal? Is forking our over $2000 dollars for two seats in the 300 section really a sound financial decision? Seriously, should I be investing time in the morning to see who the Blue Jackets and Canucks will be playing that night, in the midst of a global financial melt down? My boss once said there are 21,000 Blackhawk fans in the city of Chicago and they go to every game. It truly is an addiction fueled by wins like the one over New Jersey.

Even when the Bulls were racking up all those championships in the 90's, I still relished the chance to see the anemic Hawks. Yes, I admit, we did stink for the most part during that time. However, on any given night, no matter how low we were in the standings, you could see a great game. Some smashing good hits, a good bout or two (sometimes on the ice), speed that is unsurpassed in sports (assuming that NASCAR is not really a sport), and that euphoric feeling produced by the sight of the puck tickling the opponents twine evoked a high that is hard to duplicate. Although during that time there certainly was a lot more agony than ecstasy.

Two recent games highlighted the mercurial nature of Blackhawk hockey that leave one high as a kite or wallowing in a skid row gutter as we head to the parking lot. First off, anyone who was unfortunate enough to be in the house for the Avalanche game was intimately acquainted with the word, "Agony." Other words such as putrid, painful and pathetic come to mind. I'm reminded of that story about the little girl who, "When she was good she was very, very good. But when she was bad, she was very, very bad."

I had standing room only tickets for that stink bomb. Not only did I have to watch the debacle, I had to stand for over three hours intensifying my considerable displeasure. My daughter had a bit better luck on her seat location, getting a close up look at the pusillanimous affair. One of her friends took her and they were sitting 8 rows behind the Hawks net.

To add insult to the injury, a lady, and I use the term very loosely, spilled her beer on Taylor's coveted Toew's jersey. Not only did my little princess have to put up with the stench emanating from the ice, she had to sit in a beer soaked jersey. This almost caused a panic attack in her as we headed home. She was trying to figure out how she could wash it and not lose Captain Marvel's coveted autograph on it.

Taylor really got ticked off when the bimbo at one point exclaimed, "I thought you said these guys were good?" to whoever it was that was stupid enough to bring her. Obviously, she was not a regular, appearing to lend credence to the fact that the true fans are sitting upstairs. What a waste of a seat.

Truth be known, I had deep reservations about this game. The tussle in Boston the day before left both teams physically exhausted. Both teams lost the next day. In my opinion we don't seem to fare well in these 2pm games. My theory on why is that with Toews and Kane living without adult supervision this year, one can only imagine how late into the night their playing Playstation or face booking. We can only pray they don't discover women and beer.

If the Colorado game was the low point of the season, the game against the Devils was pure ecstasy. The Sharks game was exciting but that 2nd period against the Devils is what keeps us coming back. Speed, intensity, pace, collisions, incessant pressure and "sweet passes" as Napoleon Dynamite would say. Judd, Troy and Joel all used that tantalizing phrase, "playoff intensity," in their post game analysis. Hockey played at that level is quite simply put, exhilarating. It leaves us desperately searching for anyone who will listen to our unbridled excitement the next day.

I probably shouldn't single out any players for their contributions against New Jersey, for clearly it was a team effort. However three players stood out in my arm chair analysis. First off, when did Dave "The Basher" Bolland decide to start throwing his 180 some pounds around? I think he led the Hawks in hits that night. A little David and Goliath display.

Like most of his fellow forwards that night he used his speed to put incessant pressure on the Devils dimwitted d-men. Our "mighty mouse" did not get on the score sheet, but in my opinion had a huge impact in the favorable outcome. The slap shot he took off his skate on the penalty kill didn't seem to slow him down. Kane will become a great player when he starts to take pride in his defense like Bolland.

Next up, "To hit, or to be hit, that is the question." Our Shakespearean scholar, Niklas Hjalmarsson - yes I did have to look up how to spell his name - seemed to have a big sign on his back that said, "Crush me, I'm a Swede." Niklas paid the "price" all night chasing down loose pucks behind the net. For the most part though, his decision to get to the puck first despite the pummeling he took, led to quick departures of the puck from our zone. He was clearly the recipient of the "Beat me, whip me, make me sign bad checks," award last Friday.

Finally, the Duncster seemed to regain his pre-concussion form. Duncan seems to have a unique knack of getting to the puck a moment or two before anyone else on the ice. His quick decisions with the puck leave overzealous fore checker's dismayed and gasping for breath. I'm sure Habby and Huey would love him to play 40 minutes per game. One of Duncan's greatest accomplishments this year could be to teach Hjalmarrson how to get out of the way of the opponents suicide bombers! He may have to purchase some Rogaine after his bout with the Burrows last Sunday.

Agony and Ecstasy, living in perfect harmony, exists only in Emily Dickinson's mind. For the moment at least, I'll continue grinning like the Cheshire cat. What a ride it's been this season. Those two beautiful words, "Playoff intensity," keep echoing in my ears. At that level of play, there is not a better sport in the world.

4/5/09

"If coach would have put me in, we would have been State Champs. No doubt, no doubt in my mind." – Uncle Rico

I've had recurring nightmares since perusing Chris Block's doubt filled analysis of the Hawks post season chances at about 11:15 Friday night. The joy of clinching a playoff spot with our hard fought win over the Preds was quickly subdued while perusing his article. The thoroughly depressing read of our infinitesimal chances and past misfortune put a damper on the evening's festivities.

The hardest part for those of us that are so adept at repressing past Hawk failures is that we've played so well during stretches of this season. Have we deluded ourselves into thinking we're a legitimate contender for Lord Stanley's Cup? Are we not as good as that ineffable Flyer game on Dec. 26th? (If you recall, the frosting on the cake in that game was when Brouwer pounded Richards.) For those of you who realize Chris was dead on in his analysis, "Try to remember, those games in December!"

Doubting Chris's reservations about the Hawks chances even in round one, ("secure your tickets for home game A or B" – ouch!) are obviously backed by the statistics he's so much more familiar with than I. I indeed spent some time in the vomatorium after the first game in Chicago in the 2002 playoffs. So, do we pack it in right now? Is there a secret weapon that can get the Hawks to play with the passion necessary to advance in the playoffs wars?

I believe I have the answer. Coach Q needs to sit his players down and watch one of the greatest movies of all time, *Napoleon Dynamite*. The Hawks need to develop an Uncle Rico mindset – "No doubt in my mind." We have to be not only serious but "dead serious."

For the culture challenged Hawks fans, Uncle Rico was one of the unheralded heroes in that classic film. Largely overlooked at the Oscars, the movie was a combination of an intimate love story and the classic struggle of the underdog prevailing against insurmountable odds. Let's face it, Summer Wheatley was hot! Pedro's victory, I hope I didn't ruin this for anyone, is what gives me hope. It's the reason I'll put my head on the chopping block and predict the Hawks will glide into round two. Let's try to rebuff some of Chris's considerable concerns.

Before I go any further, I realize Chris Block has forgotten more about hockey than I know. The Hawks do resemble a Picasso more than a Rembrandt. We're never quite sure what we're going to be looking at lately. As you read my observations, which come from the heart not the brain, you'll quickly surmise I'm your typical Chicago homie. Yes, I do pick the Bears every week in the office football pool. (At least this year we have a QB who can throw the ball "about a quarter mile," as the multi-talented Uncle Rico could.)

First off, our goaltending questions appear to be a little less pressing than a few weeks ago. If we can keep Habby away from Ketel One, we should be solid at that key position. (By the way, it appears to me Habby responds with increased intensity when his name is chanted.) He will have to be a card carrying member of the Bricklayers Union if we are to advance.

Perhaps more than anyone on the team, Campbell needs to adapt to Uncle Rico's "no doubt in my mind" attitude. Jim Emilo on the post game analysis made a great observation Friday night after the Pred's game. Brian doubts his play in the d-zone so much he's starting to get lost in the o-zone, again. Brian, rush the puck up the ice more. Damn the torpedoes. Have fun out there!

Sharpie's one of those players Chris alludes to having to step up to plate. Has anyone told him lately that we don't get a goal we he bodily crosses the goal line? I haven't particularly noticed his insouciance and he's probably our best sniper. Hopefully he'll be able to fight through his injuries. On a side note, there is no doubt that Sharpie takes after Uncle Rico in the lady slaying category.

The Buffeter actually hasn't been all that bad lately. The key here is keeping his shifts short. I know we all hold out breath When Big Buff gets caught out on a long shift. Dustin needs to play "mean" and get his considerable rear end in the front of the net. Please, no stupid penalties, which usually result from getting stuck out on the ice for a prolonged period of time. It would also help if he played with a bit more emotion than Pedro displayed!

Also, kudos to Kaner for finally starting to take some interest in our defensive zone. He had a great assist on Toews' goal Friday when he fought along the boards and freed the puck up to Marvelous Martin. He must be a cog in getting our impotent power play rolling. Ultimately, Kaner's never going to be training to be a cage fighter like Napoleon's brother, Kip, but he fills a needed niche for the Hawks. Can you imagine how good Kane would be in Burrish's body?

I do believe Burrish serves a valuable purpose on this team. He's clearly a graduate at the Rex-Kwon-Do school of self defense. As Rex the sensei points out, "In Rex-Kwon-Do, we use the buddy system. No more flying solo. Someone's got your back at all times!" That describes Adam to a fault. Do you think anyone really wants to drop the gloves with "Fist Eater"? Forget about it!

Actually I've noticed Adam's skating is much improved lately. When he was boarded last Friday I told my daughter that if I was Coach Q, I wouldn't play him for the rest of the game. You just knew he was going to retaliate the first chance he got. Taylor then said, "Why doesn't Queneville just tell him not to take a dumb penalty?" I explained it to her in terms she could understand. If we leave two pounds of raw hamburger meat on the counter and tell our 105 pound Akita to be a good boy and not devour it while we run an errand, we'd probably be disappointed when we got back.

Finally, Chris clearly crossed the line when he decayed D.K. Chris, please, please never use Duncan's name in a sentence with Barker and Campbell again. That being said, I did notice our true hero coughing up the puck a lot in the first period against the Preds. However, he will be the least of out problems amongst the best players Chris alludes to that must be our best players. I don't know of a defenseman in the league who gets closer to someone's jockstrap than Keith.

Hawkhead's, is it possible that "all of our wildest dreams" could come true in June? Will we be playing tether ball like Deb and Napoleon when the movie ends? That ending was clearly one of the greatest love scenes of all time. Although I'm not sure it's the love scene the Indian staff would be attracted to, it's clearly a throwback to a time when movies were movies. Think Rhett Butler and Scarlett O'Hara. Also, note in the movie how Napoleon had Pedro's back in a crucial time. His dynamic chicken dance-electric slide-hokey pokey combo sealed the victory for Pedro. Don Cornelius, the master blaster of Soul Train, couldn't throw it down like Napoleon.

If we're going to be playing hockey for any extended period this spring, two things must occur. First we need to remember that "Passion is no ordinary word." Secondly, we need to change our slogan from "One Goal" to "Vote for Pedro!" And it wouldn't hurt to get, "dead serious."

4/22/09

DUMB AND DUMBER - give us fans an assist

After watching the Hawks thrashing of the Commie Dogs from Detroit last Saturday, I picked my daughter up from her youth group. From what I could gather, they spent the afternoon investigating the spiritual insights of suspending the lighter kids to the wall with duct tape. (Do its uses ever end?) Needless to say, she was in a bit of a goofy mood as we headed home.

As she rapidly flipped through the radio stations to find a song she liked, and I could tolerate, it happened. In a moment straight out of "*Dumb and Dumber,*" I shouted out "Taylor, we're going to a playoff game Thursday!" she screamed out "Yes, Playoffs!" She would repeat everything I said with unbridled enthusiasm. "Look out Calgary - yahoo - ride em cowboy!" Taylor started pounding on her window as if she was in front of the Plexiglas. As we continued to whip ourselves up into a piranha like frenzy I shouted, "Let's watch Miracle tonight." Immediately she responded, "Yes! Miracle, I can't wait."

When we got home, Taylor ran into the house screaming, "Mom we're going to the playoffs and we're watching Miracle tonight!" As it turned out, Nathalie was not interested in doing another in depth character study of Herb Brooks. So instead of the Coneheads, we watched *The Boy in Striped Pajama's*, which had a slightly different ending.

As a father, I can't begin to tell you how lucky I am to have a daughter who loves hockey as much as anyone who ever cleared a pond off in January. What we hockey fans lack in numbers and respect, we make up for in passion and loyalty. You had to be at the Vancouver game to see her, but to me the essence of a Hawk fan was briefly flashed on the Jumbo-Tron. Hands down, this lady should be awarded Blackhawk fan of the year.

You may recall after the near brain dead referees tried to sort out the misunderstanding that left Keith with a little less hair against Vancouver, the fellows wearing the Indian on their chest came up with an extra 4 minutes of penalties. As the ref, who may or may not have got it right, (it really doesn't matter), skated by this damsel in distress, there she was larger than life on the Tron. While cursing with clenched teeth and bated breath, she menacingly flipped "Tall Man" at the referee who had apparently just done her daddy dirty. It was an outward expression of what most of us were inwardly feeling.

The look of scorn, directed towards the visually impaired man with the orange arm band, would make Bobby Knight look like a choir boy. In an outward display of what most of us were feeling inside, it evoked a large cheer from the fans that saw her. It took one look to know this lady was the epitome of a Hawk fan. She did not need to be told when to cheer - didn't need a red towel - keep your damn bobble head - don't tell me what to wear, just get me another Goose Island. No doubt in my mind, she kicks Burrows butt in a cat fight. Why she wasn't dropping the puck at the first playoff game, I'll never know. John McDonough, you missed a golden opportunity. Cutler dropping the puck reeked of celebrity type promotions you would expect at a Bull game. (Go Derrick Rose, Go Dawg, Go!)

As the discombobulated ideas for this piece began to invade my thoughts, it occurred to me that we're seeing more and more Hispanic fans join us in the 300 level. So it was with more than a little astonishment when 4 fans of Mexican heritage sat down in the row front of me Thursday for the game. The thought occurred to me these passionate fans, (I was at the CONCAF final at Soldier field two summers ago - those fans are nuts) could be put to good use in our quest for the Cup.

First off, think piñata. Though it cost him a trip to the principal's office, Pedro's brilliant election strategy of "Smashing in the face of a piñata that resembles Summer Wheatley," sent a clear message to her and her followers. Hombres, do you think you could construct one we could take whacks at by the Hawk statue. How about a number 13 or 3 or 7? Man I'd love to bash Burrow's head in.

Actually, I enjoyed the amigo's enthusiasm as they quickly picked up the lingo of the 300 section - shoot, hit em, kill em or booing the ref. (The refs may think twice about calling a penalty if the U.C. was filled with our friends from Latin America.) In a way I envy these fans. They are not over thinking this great sport right now. Basically they just enjoy the guys in red skating fast, hitting people and occasionally dropping the gloves. (Bailar mi hermano, bailar para mi!) Watching someone like Buff or Eager try to put someone threw the boards put a huge smile on their face. They do have to work on a little hockey terminology however.

Although they'll quickly figure it out, there are no headers in hockey, although I might not put it past Fraser or Burrish. Also, they are called face offs, not "throw ins" or "corner kicks." The soccer announcer who used to scream out, "Gooooooaaaaaaalllll!!" for about a minute would be a welcome addition to the stands. There are no yellow cards, for the most part they are called two minute penalties. It's not a penalty kick, it's a penalty shot. It's an intermission, not a siesta. Finally, it is perfectly ok to call Havlat, "El Presidente!"

Occasionally, Hawk fans have been known to fuel a flickering flame. In another one of those special moments that make it worth occasionally sitting through games like the Avalanche disaster, I recall a game against the Bruins many moons ago. At the end of two the Hawks were getting their clock cleaned 4- 1. In between the second and third siesta, a tramp in a Boston jersey strolled down the aisle on top of her lame duck boy friend's shoulders. (I'm pretty sure he just got married in Iowa.) As she waved a Bruin pennant, empty beer cups were being tossed at her from every direction. I emphasize the word empty, Hawk fans are not stupid.

The boos were deafening until the fans spotted a Hawk fan carrying his girl friend on top of his shoulders. She was waving two Hawk pennants! The place went wild, giving her a standing "O." While all this bedlam was transpiring, the dumbfounded Hawks were emerging from the depths of their dismal locker room. They clearly thought the fans were exhorting them on. Responding to the cheers, the Hawks shifted gears into Stanley Cup type intensity. The Bruins never knew what hit them.

It made me reflect on us "fan-addicts" and our part in exhorting the troops down the path to the Cup. If the first two games vs. Calgary were any indication, the Hawks have a seventh man out there. Can anyone out there recall as long and raucous of a standing "O" as the one Havlat and the team got after the game tying goal in the third. The Calgary timeout immediately after the goal worked immensely to the Hawks favor as the fans just would not let the moment go. Imagine yourself as a player and listening to that! Don't tell me you wouldn't put a little extra into your next shift. A little giddy-up, in your get up and go.

Blackhawk fans, the sounds of 22,000 plus exhorting their warriors on in unison, is music to their ears. It's why a player like Ladd decided to hit anything that moved on the ice. It's why we like to go to the game and just not watch it on TV. It's the sounds of a hockey game. The "oh shit" when a cherry picker slips past our d-men. The "yes" as our net minder thwarts the breakaway. Is there anyone out there who doesn't hold their breath when there's a breakaway, and explode into joy when Captain Serious slides the puck threw the 5-hole?

It's the oohs and aahs when a puck hits the post. It's the palpable angst when the opposing goalie commits highway robbery. It's the "damn" when the puck bounces the wrong way. How about the "Yeah!" when a player gets knocked on his butt by Buff. Hopefully the Hawk brass will not try to fine tune something they really don't need to touch. Hockey fans know when to cheer, scream, toss crap on the ice, moan and groan. We don't need a "lets make some noise" sign. They know when to act like Jim Carrie and Jeff Daniels. Believe it or not, hockey fans have the highest percentage of college graduates of any sport.

So fans, as we drive home from the games singing ,*"mock - yeah, ing - yeah, bird - yeah, yeah - yeah,"* give yourselves a big assist. Hopefully our vocal cords will stand up to the test of being the greatest 7th man in hockey.

Pretty bird!

4/29/09

"And if I perish, I perish" - Queen Esther

Now I remember; it's all starting to come back to me. After 7 long years, the fog is beginning to lift; the gut wrenching anticipation, the nerves that seem impervious to the calming effect of a Goose Island Honkers Ale, the elation, depression and strained vocal cords. Having to look at the increasingly agitating opponents unshaven, toothless mugs for the 12 or so days it takes to complete a series or listening to the amplified sounds of the crowd as they realize the do or die situation.

We also start to see sports writers coming out of the woodwork as they finally realize where that noise on the west side of the city is emanating from. A time where every square inch of ice is contested, vigorously. A time when we pray our net minder becomes the 8th wonder of the world. All of this accompanied by hitting that rivals the "Thrilla in Manilla." And now, as we enter the Conference semi's we have to ratchet it up another notch! Forget the players, does anyone realize the exhausting effect a series has on the fans?

Although it might be sacrilegious to say, it might not even be the Cup we are clamoring for. I believe hockey fans just have a very hard time letting the season end. We long to see one more game, one more period, one more shot, one more bout or one more hit that leaves a player's spouse running to increase her husband's life insurance policy. My daughter perfectly described the dilemma as we drove home from the final regular season game against the Pred's last year.

As we headed home, just short of grabbing the 8 hole in the playoffs, Taylor asked me, "Dad, what am I going to do for the next 4 months?" It takes a while to adjust to baseball's casual pace. While I'd stop short of comparing our craving to that of a heroin addict, when you get a taste of playoff hockey, the reluctance of seeing the season come to an end is multiplied exponentially.

I could pick from a boat load of plays in the Calgary series, yet one incident epitomized the essence of what it takes to advance in the playoffs in my non technical mind. Brian Campbell and Warren Peters were in a race to see who could get to a puck along the right dashboards in the 3rd period last Saturday. Brian, who the Hawk organization did not draft to be a "Hit Man," and the Flame player collided like two atoms in a particle accelerator at the Fermi Labs. It was the classic example of the irresistible force meeting the immovable object. Both players ended up flying backwards, dusting off their britches after shaking the cobwebs out a bit.

It was the type of courage that reminds me of the Old Testament character, Queen Esther. In one of the bravest acts recorded in the Bible, Esther was willing to take one for the team. She was willing to put her head on the chopping block in an effort to thwart the vile Haman's plans. Approaching King Xerxes, without being summoned was sure to be awarded the death penalty. After her Uncle Mordecai urges her to throw caution to the wind, she utters 6 of the most memorable words in the Bible, "And if I perish, I perish."

Now I realize it's a stretch, and Campbell's collision did not save a nation. However, what knowledgeable fan can deny that plays like that have a profound effect on the outcome of a game? Teams whose players are willing to "perish" in the corners end up playing for the Stanley Cup. Those that don't, head for the Links.

My part in the perishing scenario has been taking the dogs for walks after midnight, as the rest of my family scurries for the cover and warmth of their beds. When we lost I have to admit, the walk was a begrudging one. I certainly didn't mind going the extra mile with the beasts when we triumphed! Saturday night I actually came up with an idea for naming our much maligned 4rth line.

First off, have you ever noticed how a dog can put his nose inches away from a pile of poop, investigating the smells as if the mysteries of the universe are unfolding? I've come to the conclusion that Burrish and the rest of his pack just like investigating the pile ups in front of the net. Some thoughts occurred to me for possible names for this hardworking line. The "Don't dog me," "Knucklehead," "Pooper Scooper" and "Slime ball," lines were all possibilities. My favorite though would be "The Nozzle Line." It just seems to fit. The energy line is just too polished for the likes of Eager, Burrish and Brouwer.

I can't think of too many players I'd be less "eager" to go into a corner with than Gentle Ben. Brouwer, with his bad boy playoff beard, is fitting in nicely after spending most of the season with our pretty boys. I'm pretty sure Phaneuf is still trying to figure out if he was hit by a train or fell off a barn. Although I have forbid my daughter to seek his autograph, Burr-dog is loudly turning into "The Total Package." Against the Flames he hit, won face offs, instigated and most importantly, stayed out of the "dog house." Although Adam tried his hand at shoulder surgery on Rene Borque, I doubt Dr.Terry, the team orthopedic physician, will have to be too concerned about losing his job. Dr. Fist Eater continues to work without anesthetics, adhering to his personal motto, "Feel the pain!"

In my mind there are two players on the Hawks who should not choose to perish, yet. Havlat should only go into the corners with heavy cover. Patrick Kane, who's been a constant target of post game calls this year on the radio, needs to remain healthy. Fans call in complaining, "Kane needs to get tough," or "He needs to become a two way player," or "He needs some maturity," – (this one usually after Kane high sticked someone when they tried to kill him). Hawkhead's, do we realize we have a 20 year old kid who just compiled his second 70 point season!

Sorry fans, Kaner will never be a Burr-dog. However I believe he was quite effective in the Calgary series, especially the last two games. The kid has a nose for the net. What Hawk would you rather see with the puck on his stick on the power play? Perhaps all we need to do is get him on Buffy "The Flame Slayers" diet.

I'm sure the hockey pundits could come up with a few backline tandems, but Keith and Seabrook could become a Hawk defensive pair that fans will be talking about 20 years from now. The poor fools who choose to perish on Captain Crunch's side are thinking there has to be an easier way to make a living. If you choose to try to invade are zone along the starboard side, you will get hit, rigorously. Duncan just tends to pick your pocket, more of an Oliver Twist approach to defense. I believe they are the heart of this team. Iginla will probably require mental therapy after reoccurring nightmares of seeing Duncan Keith in his face.

As we enter round two in the quest for the Cup, the hair pulling Canucks will be well rested after their quick dispatch of the Blues. (Take heart Hawkhead's, we are not the Blues.) Yet another West Coast team, meaning more groggy mornings and late night walks with the dogs. It might be wise for Coach Q to have his players shave their heads, severely limiting Vancouver's ruffians. Bring on the Burrows piñata's! I do know one thing; if we want to advance into a match up with Anaheim, (yuk, yuk), the Hawks will have to take a Queen Esther approach when they head into the corners. The Canucks will never know what hit em!

When it all comes down to it, I just don't want this season to end!

5/7/09

Fetch the Sledge Rufus

As we forged are way through the clogged arteries towards the expressway after Tuesday's excruciatingly painful affair, Taylor asked me the inevitable question. "Dad, what was wrong with us tonight?" For once, I found myself at a loss for words to even begin to describe whatever it was that had just transpired at the United Center.

If John McDonough was serious about turning this organization around, he would have had the ushers handing out refunds as we exited the building. As we trudged out, one was overcome with a feeling similar to a dismal bowel movement. Borrowing a line from Dilbert "Sandpapering your body and then rolling in salt," would probably be an improvement to watching that contest.

However, in the semi-immortal words of Alfred E. Neuman - "What, me worry?" Sorry all you knowledgeable critics, you'll have to excuse me if I don't get down on my knees and worship a bunch of goofball lumberjacks yet. As we discovered in Games 1 and 2, their spiritual leader, the great Italian goaltender Roberto Luongo, is not infallible. Did he really need to trash talk my man Buff after the game Tuesday? If I were Dustin I'd load up on some refried beans and pork tenderloin before game 4. I think the air around Roberto's crease needs to be freshened up a bit!

While they all made salient points, the announcers could not have sounded more depressed if they tried, during the post game analysis. If I heard "Vancouver executed their game plan" one more time, I was going to drive my car into the back of a semi-truck on the Dan Ryan. Do you really think those morons have a game plan? And if they did they could remember what it was; please!

Here's my game plan – get the puck to the net, work hard along the boards, skate fast, get back, finish checks and look for rebounds. Sounds a bit familiar doesn't it? If the truth be known, the Canucks just plain and simple had a step on us all night. Actually, I believe their game plan consisted of two parts;

1. Putting 22,000 people to sleep.

2. Having 5 players stand in front of Luongo, hoping he would be able to stop anything that managed to get by the herd of caribou grazing in front of his net.

Pardon my frustration, but after watching the Wing/Duck epic on Sunday afternoon, Tuesday's game was indigestible. It was a complete dud, a water logged fire cracker. The players in the Wing/Duck game were skating as fast in the 3rd overtime as they were in the 1st period. Up and down, fast paced, hard hitting hockey for 6 periods. Now don't get me wrong, I believe the Hawks were trying to put forth an effort. Brouwer had 8 hits and Buff had 9. It just seemed to be a case of being a dollar short and a day late all night. A writer in the Tribune described it best – "skating uphill."

In my opinion, Kesler should have received the games first star. Before the game I really wanted to see Burrows flattened like a crepe. It took all of about 20 seconds to redirect my angst and antipathy towards # 17, truly a nozzle extraordinaire. Kesler's pass to Raymond was one that very few players in the NHL make. Nine out of ten players would have shot that puck immediately. The skillful agitator waited, taking a huge hit from Byfuglien in the process, (again, a day late and a dollar short), before feathering one of the prettiest passes I've seen all year to the Flash. That was the play of the game in my book.

As co-founder and president of the Duncan Keith Admiration Society, I have to admit, I'm dumbfounded at the number of times Duncan has fallen to the ground without getting clobbered. Double rudders were not out of the question on Tuesday. Part of the problem is that our expectations of Keith are so high, his rare miscues are greatly magnified. Chris Block noted in the Calgary series that Keith may be nursing an undisclosed injury to his left foot. Of course, only he and his hair dresser know for sure – neither he or the team is divulging any information.

Hawk fans, you really need to pick it up a level. If the play on the ice was lethargic, the 7th man appeared to be taking a nap. Could it be that there are a lot of fans who just jumped on the bandwagon at this crucial juncture of the season? Corporations entertain a lot of people that I suspect would be looking for cake when icing is called. Forget the dessert cart already. Just prior to the Hawks taking the ice, lets start a "Lets go Hawks" cheer. Let them hear you in the locker room. You want the Hawks to score first, prove it! (Unfortunately, I realize anyone reading this is probably not the problem.) And here I thought the "frozen chosen," only hung out in church on Sunday morning – can I get an "amen" Hawk fans!

Back to Taylor's question – "What was wrong with us?" (Have you ever noticed how we speak in terms of us or we, as if were an extension of the warriors on the ice?) In an "attempt" to explain what went wrong, I was reminded of an old comic strip that was called, "*Gasoline Alley.*" Now those were the days comics were comics! There were two old characters in the comic strip named Joel and Rufus. Not the sharpest knives in the drawer, but they knew how to get the job done.

When anything broke down and required "fixin," Joel's answer to the problem was quite simple. "Fetch the sledge, Rufus!" Actually it sheds some light on what we need to do next game; we have to just keep hammering away in other words. Hammering the corners, hammering the crease, nailing the faceoff's and sledge hammering those objects of wrath otherwise known as Burrows and Kesler. Don't forget to keep hammering shots at the trash talker in the net. Although it's been said the devils in the details, a lot of hockey just comes down to "fetchin the sledge."

So ye of little faith take heart! I have a very good feeling going into tonight's game. Nathalie made an awesome pork roast last night. One might be inclined to say, "All systems are go!"Let's not coronate the Nucks yet, let's hammer them. Buff, lets make Luongo put on a gas mask tonight. If I can borrow a line from the movie *Apocalypse Now*, "I love the smell of pork roast in the morning. It smells like victory!"

5/11/09

In Spring Time a Young Mans Fancy Turns to...

Hockey? Perhaps REM was right; it is the end of the world as we know it. It feels strange walking into the U. C. as we approach mid May. Normally a season of amorous pursuit, 22,000 maniacs can still be heard screaming for blood on West Madison Street. The fairer sex is well represented in that total. There's just something a little different about a Blackhawk woman. A bit rough around the edges, there's an innate beauty in their passion and love of violence.

Watching the Hawk players hugging each other, while they celebrate after goals, has caused me a little consternation lately. I'm a bit concerned by the phobia ridden possibilities but..., would it be wrong for two men in Bob Probert jerseys to hug each other if we clinch tonight? I'm not saying it will happen, but you might feel compelled to morph into a wild and crazy guy after we dispatch the Canucks.

If you do, one would be well advised to view the "Man Hug," video on you-tube. "Tilt head to the left, don't think about touching necks, do not touch chests under any circumstances, butts must stick out, pat each other firmly 3 times on the back and break immediately." The break is crucial in the man hug. It must be clean and instantaneous. No Lingering!

Now that we have the gay alert out of the way, (I was a Boy Scout, always be prepared.), was game 4 a rush or what?! Tina Turner could not have taken us higher. I'm quite sure anyone in attendance is scrambling to get tickets to tonight's affair. Good luck. Game 6 tickets will have to be handled with asbestos gloves. I Got Mine!

Is it just me, or are the playoffs starting to wear you down? Throughout the season, starting seriously about late February, Taylor and I have tried to figure out how to get to every next game. Hopefully some psychiatrist 10 years from now will not be accusing her of enabling her dad's addiction. You know you're in trouble when you look earnestly into each others eyes, knowingly saying, "That Columbus game is going to be a big one!"

Sam Fels, the Committed Indian editor whose self portrait is on page two of the Committed Indian, (Don't enter the U. C. without it), described the rush we Hawk fans crave, in an article a few months back. He reminisced about a come from behind victory over the Blues at the old Stadium. Apparently, all the horses escaped from the barn that day – it was a wild one. After the game, which was standing room only, one of his older brothers friends hoisted Sam above his head and was ready to throw him to the ice as an apparent sacrifice of thanksgiving. Thankfully he didn't go through with it or we would have no C.I. to peruse before each game. Thanks Sam, they've really added to this season.

The rushes from the last two games have left me with fits of intermittent sleep the last few days. If there were any new fans present after Game 4, I'm pretty sure they will be back. We'll have to humor them while they scream, "Shoot, hit em, you stink ref etc.," until they can become more knowledgeable about the game. (Actually, after almost 50 years, those shouts still occasionally come out of my mouth.) Do you think the Hawk players could here you screaming, "Let's go Hawks," as we filed down the hallways and stairwells on cloud nine!

Besides the lack of sleep, I'm not sure how much longer my internal constitution can take of Playoff pandemonium. I was sitting on the edge of my seat at a friend's house Thursday, rocking back and forth, moving side to side, with every shot or check. My finger nails are approaching their cuticles. Will I be able to hold up for another series? As I approach 60, perhaps a Gay and Lesbian poetry slam would be more my speed. Roses are red, violets are blue, it's time to send Vancouver, back to the zoo.

As Jeff Beck sang many moons ago, "I ain't superstitious, but a black cat just crossed my trail." Am I rowing this boat alone, or are some of you doing superstitious things right now to help the Hawks. I ate at one of the great Hawk head hangouts before game 3 in a little Italian joint called Tufano's. After Rocky Marciano, err I mean Joey sat us, it occurred to me that the last time I ate there, the Hawks lost. I had already ordered, and one of my favorite pre-game meals before the Hawk games (the shrimp, broccoli and shells) was on its way. As I stared at the great sport pictures on the wall by the bar, I did my best to convince myself that eating at Tufano's has no impact on the outcome of what transpires on the ice at the U.C. (Joey, I'm sorry, but I'm not going to risk game six. I will be back for the next round!)

The rest of you superstitious cats, don't throw away your lucky penny, rabbits foot and gypsy ring yet. Are you growing a playoff beard? I know RoseLee will have on her sparkling Hawks broach. Do you watch the game at the same saloon or house? Where the same unwashed clothes? Sit in the same chairs and insist everyone else does to? (Arla, I'm talking about you here.) Have you been eating refried beans and pork roast since that was the meal that you ate before Game 4? My daughter is getting tired of it and yesterday finally had enough. "I wish people would stop farting in this house," she exclaimed after I broke wind one to many times.

Enough of that nonsense, time to give you my "analytical" synopsis of the series, especially the last two games. I'm convinced we're the better team, although I'm now well aware of what Luongo can do. Fortunately, the goalie no one wanted this year, has been just as brilliant. I've come to the conclusion that we don't need a sixth attacker if things are getting dicey at the end of the game. Habby has shown us far too often in this series that he wants to join the attack!

Our version of the "Bruise Brothers," Buff and Gentle Ben, most certainly are causing insomnia amongst the Vancouver hopefuls. Simply put, they have brutalized our opponent, giving us the slight edge in the series. Although it has been said that it's impossible to give more than 100%, Dustin and Eager are playing at about 110%. They seem to be taking a sadistic joy in the pain they are inflicting on our adversaries.

Sharp, Ladd and Brouwer also have contributed mightily to the Hit Parade. I've said it before and I'll say it again, hard hits in the corners lead to goals. They take a toll over the course of a series. My brother's roommate Matt has been clamoring for more ice time for the "Nozzle Line." The pooper scoopers, Burrish, Brouwer and Eager, have been a royal pain in the butt the whole series.

Although he hasn't appeared much on the score sheet, I just love the way Toews is working behind the net at both ends. El Presidente has been magnificent. There's not enough room to talk about our backline contributions. I'll only mention that Campbell needs to keep carrying the puck and continue to wonder why anyone would want to goad Walker into a fight. It seems anyone who has been foolish enough to dance with Matt has paid the price this year. You might say he has two left feet. More than your feet will get stomped on.

The biggest fight of either of the first two series has been who gets to go to the game when our turn in the rotation comes up for our two season tickets. Before game 3 it was determined that Taylor and I would go to the first game, with Nathalie and Greg getting Game 4. Not even 5 minutes passed after the Game 3 disaster before Taylor shifted into an aggressive lobbying mode. "Dad we need to be there. We're the real fans. Mom goes there to socialize and Greg will just talk the whole game." (Neither of her assessments was entirely accurate, but desperate times call for desperate measures.)

When I finally told her, "Taylor, we have to be fair, it's there turn," she came up with a ploy that even caught me off guard. "Ok then, how about you drop Greg and I off at the U.C.?" That really made me chuckle. Taylor and Greg can't sit in the car next to each other for 5 minutes without driving me crazy.

I nixed this desperate, but ingenious attempt by Taylor, because I'm afraid Sam Fels would throw one of them unto the ice before the final horn.

One other fight ensued yesterday at my moms. My brother Bob, who was in on our season ticket package, had the two tickets for Game 6. He offered to take me to tonight's game, which could turn out to be the hottest ticket to a Chicago sports event this year. Taylor immediately said, "Why should you get to go, and not me?" (How about I paid for the tickets and organized our season ticket consortium!) In her mind, the best fan should get to go.

My brother John was really ticked off. 'I'm not going to watch the game tonight. I'm going to TP both yours and Bob's house. I told him, "John, our Akita will be chained to a tree in the front yard. He has a long leash!" (John texted me from my house when the Star Spangled Banner was playing that night and said the dogs were enjoying their steaks!)

In closing, I know a lot more about the Canucks than I did a year ago. Their dog breath defensemen are quite talented. Johnson, Rypien and Kesler have really impressed me. Actually, Vancouver is a beautiful city. There is a road from the city to Whistler, where the next winter Olympics will be contested. The road runs along the breathtaking Howe Sound.

About half way up to Whistler there is a golf course that had the most spectacular views of any course I've ever hacked up. I recall shooting an 89, despite losing 6 balls. I had to play the last hole quite cautiously. I was down to my last ball, which had a red stripe around it. Hopefully, the Canuck players will take some solace tomorrow on that course. The views from the tee boxes make you forget about everything.

Hit em straight!

Although I've thrown quite a few, I've never been to a Clincher! Please don't forget to view the man hug video. Remember, absolutely no lingering!

5/15/09

Carpe Diem

Hanging from what appears to be the first row in the 200 level, the large white sheet had three simple words hastily painted in red. If you still have your 2008-09 pocket schedules, open it and take a gander. The first time I saw it, I thought to myself that it perfectly captured the essence of the Blackhawk revival. It's a revival that actually started last year. Think about it, had you ever seen fans so passionate about a team that didn't make the playoffs in Chicago history?

There were several teams last year that breathed a sigh of relief when we were finally eliminated. The standing room only crowd at the last home game gave the never say die warriors a spine tingling ovation as the game and season wound down. Three simple words on that old white sheet told the story of the 2007-08 season - Pride is Back.

Even though this year has been phenomenal, last year was a space in time that will never be duplicated. With crowds initially averaging 10000 to 12000 fans, you could buy a seat in the Boonies for $10 the day of the game. It was by far the greatest deal in professional sports. The Hawks were flying under the radar as the renaissance grew roots. Then Dennis Savard had to open his big mouth in a post game tirade, uttering four more simple words that will be in Blackhawk lore forever, "Commit to the Indian!" All the sudden the house started filling up - Pride is back.

The pride was fueled by many young players who were too green to know that their time had not yet come. Anyone who has followed the Hawks over the years innately sensed we had something special percolating in the mausoleum that had been Blackhawk hockey. And it wasn't just Batman and Robin, aka Toews and Kane. There was an infusion of speed, team chemistry, an indomitable spirit, not to mention a growing passion in the fans who exhorted them on. It was quite clear - Pride is Back.

So should we be surprised when Duncan Keith is quoted after the Vancouver series saying, "We haven't won anything yet." Surely the Hawks, after winning two hard fought series in the playoffs, could easily be satisfied with what they have accomplished thus far. I think on anyone's radar screen this will be remembered as a season that has exceeded our expectations.

However, is it realistic to expect this team to advance to the Stanley Cup Finals? If the truth be known, the other teams left are said to be a notch above us. Yet, I think the warriors who wear the Indian Head on their chest have started to set their aim a bit higher. As Robert Browning noted, "Ah but a man's reach should exceed his grasp, or what's a heaven for?" We appear to be becoming "the Little Engine that thought he could team." Chugging along that uphill track - Pride is back.

In a past article this year entitled, "You might be a Blackhawk fan if..." I mentioned that not all true fans sit in the 300 section. I pointed out an "Older Couple" who I've seen at just about any Hawk game I've ever attended. Through a round about way, we contacted each other, and it has been a delight corresponding with RoseLee, 81, and Earl, 83, as the season progressed. They have been attending games since 1952! Earl stated the only mistake he's made in their marriage was taking RoseLee to her first game.

Apparently she fell for the Hawks hook, line and sinker. It should be noted, with great pride I might add, that in the early years they spent some time in the sacred grounds of the Stadiums second balcony! RoseLee also noted, "At that time you could walk up to a ticket window and buy a ticket the day of a game." Sounds a bit familiar, doesn't it? Currently it's tough to find a seat at the U.C. - Pride is Back.

No one was more excited than RoseLee and Earl when the Hawks clinched on Monday. "Well, will there ever be a night as exciting as this last one ...All the nights going home feeling drained and dismal were perhaps good for us, since we were able to feel so fabulous in remembering the comparisons," wrote RoseLee. When I mentioned I was going to write about their loyalty she perfectly summarized it for me; "...its sort of hard to distinguish between loyalty and love for us...maybe you can't have one without the other."

RoseLee wrote that no matter what happens, the Hawks have exceeded expectations and rewarded to the core, old timers like themselves. I guarantee you; the "Older Couple" may say their satisfied with the season, but in their hearts it's only just begun. Ah to dream the impossible dream. I really think the patriarch and matriarch of Blackhawk hockey should be dropping the ceremonial puck in the first game of the 4th series! Many moons ago the Hawks were a once proud organization - Pride is Back.

Although I loathed him for most of the series, my heart went out to Roberto Luongo after the shoot out at the OK Corral last Monday. I heard he was near tears as he blamed himself for the loss. "Seven goals; I did not get the job done," he lamented. However, anyone of the 40 players who battled each other in Game Six could walk off the ice with their heads held high. There is no such thing as defeat if you've left it all on the ice. As it was said of the French Foreign Legion "They were never defeated. They were only killed."

Actually that night I saw a picture of a painting RoseLee did of Keith Magnuson as he tried to deal with the heartbreaking loss of the Hawks in the 7th game of the 1971 Stanley Cup Finals. Henri Richard, the "Pocket Rocket," had eluded Keith's all out diving attempt to stop him before he deposited the game winning goal. The picture of Maggie is the one on the cover of this book. Gaze at the picture and you'll quickly see there's a lot more to this game than money. As we watched the combatants exchange handshakes, (clearly one of the best traditions in pro sports), the 22,000 plus in attendance realized - Pride is Back.

This young group of Hawks seems to be realize what it means to slip that red sweater over their heads. To digress just for a moment, I'd like to bring up another Chicago athlete who in a 1965 Sports Illustrated article was touted as one of 10 can't miss players in the NBA draft. They said of the player known as the Evansville Hustler, "He's not fast, ok shot and can't jump very well." Why this player would make the NBA with that mediocre assessment was summarized in the next sentence – "He'll make it on his hustle."

Jerry Sloan took the most pride in his defense. If we are to hoist and drink out of the greatest trophy in sports it will boil down to hustle and elbow grease. It's why a player like Adam Burrish is playing in the NHL. It's why an opposing team hates to see "The Nozzle Line," jump over the boards for their shift. There's only one way to advance in the playoffs, the old fashioned way, you earn it. When it comes to paying the price - Pride is Back.

As my ramblings draw to a close I'd like to mention a commercial that seems to epitomize us hockey fans. It's the one where a dad is in the nursery screaming while banging on the window as if it were Plexiglas, "You own this nursery!" He then points at every other baby, whom he's presumably just woke up, pointing his finger at each one of them shouting, "Loser, loser, loser." After banging one more time on the glass he looks at his kid and exclaims, "Best baby in the world!" Who can deny our baby Hawks have made us proud. Best team in the NHL! -Pride is Back.

RoseLee and Earl, I think the best is yet to come. There will be a night as exciting as last Monday. For those of us over 50, it might be a wise idea to find the locations of the heart resuscitators in the U.C. There's a song by one of my favorite bands that has been played a few times at the U.C. this year. It's by Robert Bradley's Blackwater Surprise group. I love the line in that song that goes, "Tell me what, is going on, in Big City?" I'll tell you what – Pride is Back.

The War Drums in the Distance are not so muffled anymore. It's clearly time to "Seize the Day!"

5/24/09

HIGH HOPES and HAPPY WAYS

"Just what makes that little old ant,
think he can move that rubber tree plant,
Any one knows an ant, can't,
move a rubber tree plant."

Some of you may know the next line to the classic *"High Hopes,"* sung by Frank Sinatra. Hope is close to all we have to cling to at the moment, hope and a wing and a prayer. If you recall the Hawks opened on the road this year, getting spanked first by the Rangers, then by the Capitols. My daughter went into a full blown panic attack. "Dad, are we going to be ok, what's wrong with us?"

The hype leading into the season had raised the expectations to not just getting into the playoffs, but to be one of the dominant teams in the NHL. I'm not sure I convinced her when I told her to chill out, that we'd certainly win a game before the 82 game season concluded. (While I didn't admit it, at that point I was a little concerned myself!)

"Are we going to be ok now," after Detroit has taken a 2-0 lead in the series, is a much tougher question. It's one that seems to have been answered by the pragmatic sports writers and doomsayers – we're pretty much dead as a door nail. They've even thrown the first few shovels of dirt on top of the grave. We've all heard repeatedly that the Wings are too good to lose 4 out of their next 5 games. The statistic that says a team who takes a 2-0 lead wins 85% of the time is not particularly encouraging. However, being the brain dead homey I am, I'm going to go out on a very slim, tenuous limb. I predict we'll choose to focus on that 15% of the time. Think about it a minute; wouldn't you love to be getting 15% in your bank account.

I realize the vultures are circling. In addition, the hockey savants and pessimistic fans claim to know as John Donne wrote, "For whom the bell tolls." Yet miracles do happen. Duncan Keith awhile back was quoted, "Positive thinking brings positive results." Think Miracle on Ice, Think Karate kid or Aquila and the Bee." Think Rocky 1-15! If the truth be known, this series actually is a microcosm of Communism vs. Truth, Justice and the American Way. Who can deny, with there commie red uniform and tremendous ability, that the Red Wings more closely resemble those dominant Russian teams lead by Tretiak.

On paper, Hope vs. Skill does not seem to be a fair battle. It seems to be in the recesses of our human nature that we cling to the pestilences that emerged from Pandora's box, rather than the one positive item – Hope. Pessimism – woe is me, Death – quite sudden as it was Tuesday, Disease – as we note the debilitating injuries that are hobbling our stars, Fault Finding – also known as the blame game, and Searing Pain – after game 2, knowing that's one that got away, are far easier to embrace than hope. However, I ask you who are old enough to remember; did repeated failures to pull a rabbit out of his hat ever stop Bullwinkle J. Moose?

Tuesdays night gut wrenching defeat left one completely enveloped by a heavy moroseness. As Snoopy from Charlie Brown would begin to describe it, "It was a dark and stormy night." Talk about a debilitating loss. I was left with a similar feeling to a game two years ago where the Hawks completely dominated a game shots and hits wise, but lost on a last second counter punch in OT. As I drove home with 3 young kids in the car, I couldn't take the analysts pessimism any longer and stated, "We deserved to win that game," finally angrily shutting off the radio.

Now all 3 kids have a different version of my reaction, but we all know how kids exaggerate! The little imps claim I violently punched the radio button and let out an expletive uncharacteristic of a Children's Church leader. From that time on, my son Greg always asks if I'm going to punch the radio if the Hawks lose. If I were in a car on Tuesday night, I probably would have head butted the dashboard. It's kind of like throwing a golf club; it does nothing to help the situation. Yet, sometimes it is our only defense when we are, as the famous golf writer Bernard Darwin described us, "the dogged victims of inexorable fate."

In game two we truly fought with a passion and intensity that should have been rewarded with a "W." That old blues song, "Everybody wanna win, nobody wanna lose," does have a ring of truth to it, yet if I could see 82 games a year played with that speed, excitement and intensity, I wouldn't complain. It was a great game to watch. Don't tell me 20000 fans in the "Joe" did not start panicking when Capt. Serious tied it up. The sudden drop of air pressure after the Commie dogs won it in overtime was due to the Wing fans finally breathing again.

The game was fiercely contested with both goalies taking an extremely active part in the evening's festivities. (i.e. – they were standing on their heads for the most part.) Both Habby and Ozzie resembled one of those pistachio nuts that are only partially cracked open. You know the kind of nut where you wonder what's going to give first, the nut or your finger nail. Actually the Hawks transitioned out of the d-zone much better than game one, giving Detroit a dose of their own foul tasting medicine. It's amazing how much easier that is when you're not standing around. Scoring chances were abundant.

Kane looked much more aggressive, although he may want to try to quit stick handling between 4 Wings, (otherwise known throughout the league as the Versteegian technique). As the sagacious Chris Block noted, sometimes less is more. Sometimes you just have to let the "chip ins," fall where they may. As Coach Babcock noted, "Kane looked like he was having fun out there." (On a totally unrelated side note, didn't it always appear Walter Payton was having fun out there? I miss # 34 and his boundless enthusiasm.)

Although it's a good barometer of a players two way game, I think the plus/ minus statistic in this series has been over hyped. The players, who were on the ice for a couple of rare miscues by our defense corps, didn't really deserve a minus in my estimation. After winning two face offs did Toews really deserve a minus? Did Brouwer deserve a minus for hustling back, coming within inches of the puck before Samuelson closed his eyes, said a quick Hail Mary, and shot.

Brian Campbell did earn his minus point in game two though. Before going any further, I want to make it abundantly clear that I think Soupy has been fantastic in the playoffs, our best d-man by far. My thought on the pass was if he had managed to connect with Barks (who was drooling like a dog in anticipation), we would have had a considerable number advantage at the net for a redirect or banging home a rebound past the pistachio nut in the net. It appeared 3 Wing forwards were putting pressure on the perimeter.

Campbell went from hero to zero in the blink of an eye. As Chris Block pointed out, it might have not been Coach Q's smartest decision to put Brian right back out there after a 45 second shift in OT. My thought is Coach Q was going for the jugular, giving us two excellent options on the blue line. My advice to Brian – listen to a song by Joe Walsh and The Barnstomers called *Happy Ways*. The last verse has some very sound advice;

"Then something happens, seems to go bad,
Cancel the feeling and look towards the sky,
No need to worry bout consequences,
Give it a giggle instead of a sigh."

For us Hawk fans, watching the three red Commies come barreling down the pipe towards the last bastion of democracy in our nets, is a scene that somehow we will have to erase from our memory banks. You could almost hear the robot from Lost in Space exclaiming, "Danger, danger, Will Robinson, Aliens approaching!"

In closing, we do appear to be floating in a barrel about 1000 feet from Niagara Falls right now. Detroit seems to have stuck a dagger in us in game 2. It reminds me of an 11-12 year old girls softball game a few years back and a statement made by my assistant coach. Trying to exhort our players on he hollered, "We got the dagger in them, now we need to twist it!" (I did ask him to run his motivational speeches by me before passing them on to the team in the future.) The Wings still have some twisting to do.

Generally speaking, people smiling while the world crumbles around them are prime candidates for that little yellow bus. Yet, I'm extremely optimistic about tonight's game. If we get the same effort out of our warriors that we did on Tuesday, well could we ask for anything more? Let the "chip ins" fall where they may. Although some of you might not understand "all systems are go," again this morning. Diehards in sections 321 – 326 we need you tonight, lets hear those battle cries! Throughout the season I've noticed you've led the charge all year. Let's rock that joint on West Madison Street.

It's time to "cancel the feeling" of game two's series of unfortunate events.

"So any time you're getting low,
Stead of letting go
Just remember that ant
Oops there goes another rubber tree plant!"

Believe in Miracles. Hey Rocky, want to watch me pull a rabbit out of my hat. Move the queen out. Spell your butt off. Start wailing on those sides of beef in the freezer! Vote for Pedro!

Adrian, Adrian!

5/28/09

36

Quiet Desperation

"Hey Chris, do we have any aces up our sleeve for tonight's game?"
– Rich Lindbloom

"Go Fish." – Chris Block

About 12 years ago I was walking our two Akita's around the lake across from our house with my 4 year old daughter. It was a "winter's day, in a deep and dark December," as Paul Simon would put it. The lake had frozen over and we walked up to an ice fisherman drinking a cold one, while staring into a hole in the ice.

Taylor, with a curious look upon her face, asked me what the man was doing. I explained to her that he was ice fishing, hoping to catch the one that got away. We said hello and investigated the site for a moment, before I said, "C'mon Tay, lets go." 'Wait dad, I want to watch him catch a fish," she replied. Both the fisherman and I had a good laugh before he stated, "Honey, you'll probably be here awhile!" Lo and behold, within minutes, the fisherman hauled in a nice size trout. Ah, to have the faith of a child. Indeed my Lord, let the little children come.

Obviously, we Hawk fans are leading "lives of quiet desperation" as Thoreau so eloquently put it. Down 3-1, the prospects of catching the multi-talented Wings are clearly obfuscated by reality. As I beat my head against a wall Sunday night after the Wings spanked us, repeating over and over, "Chris Block is right, Chris Block is right," it was hard to find any consolation from the disarray that took place hours earlier at the U.C. One of my friends daughters who has really been smitten by the Blackhawk bug, asked me at one point why Detroit had no goalie in there net. I did my best to explain what a delayed penalty was. However, I probably should have just told her the Wings were trying to make it fair. It was that bad. Welcome to Blackhawk hockey Catherine. It's a love affair with many peaks and valleys.

Even RoseLee, the 81yr old matriarch of the Hawks noted rather begrudgingly, "Heart knowledge is not head knowledge." The following lines from Alexander Pope concisely summarize those of us who follow the Hawks with our hearts;

"The ruling passion, be it what it will,
The ruling passion conquers reason still.

Chris Block is firmly grounded in reality, while I steadfastly cling to the slim hope of comeback of momentous proportions. RoseLee wrote me about a time when her boys were in Little League. After a bad game, rather than focus on the dropped fly ball or called third strike, they'd try to concentrate on the one or two positive plays that took place. For two days now, I've tried to find something positive, that would give me even a glimmer of hope, to no avail.

In a desperate moment I e-mailed Chris B. and asked him, what he thought about bringing Akim Aliu up. Chris has been pretty high on his skills all year so I thought maybe this is a trump card we have at our disposal. I guess this would come under the heading of "grasping for straws."

Although Chris refrained from saying, "I told you so," he did point out another loose cannon on the ice is not the answer. About the most positive statement I've gotten from Chris during this fantastic playoff run was, "I don't know how, but they just keep on winning." Even I whose heart screams, "Never say die," must admit the glass is half empty. Does the season end as T.S Eliot described the world's plight?

"This is the way the world ends
Not with a bang but a whimper."

Can this ineffable season really end on such a disconsolate note? If it were the Ducks, it would be a little less painful, but to lose in this fashion to the hated Red Wings? The best way I could possibly describe Sunday's rout would be to compare it to taking a huge swig of sour milk out of a carton. (By the way, trust me, you'll do that one time and smell every carton of milk you ever drink from again.) It takes quite awhile to get that taste out of your mouth. Somehow, the Hawks have to put the foul taste of Sunday's thrashing behind them.

While I'll finally concede Detroit is the better team on paper, they're not that much better. I challenge you to follow the rambling thoughts of a desperado, in an attempt to plug the ever enlarging hole in the dike. Here is my 10 point plan to save the season;

1. Reunite "The Nozzle Line." I don't know why, but I really liked the chemistry of Brouwer, Eager and Burrish. (I know C.B. will probably go back and find out they were a minus 6 when paired together.) If nothing else it would probably elicit an "Oh no not those douche bags again," when they jumped over the boards.

2. Put Sharp back on a line with Toews and Kane. What we give up in true grit we gain in knowing all three of these forwards are adept at putting the puck in the net. Have Kane review the movie, "Revenge of the Nerds."

3. Give our d-men a crash course in French. Teach them how to say, "Save my but again, Cristobal," or "Remember the Bastille!" I'd also recommend that Huet keep smiling. Have you noticed how much fun he appeared to be having this year when he was playing well? Expect a momentous performance that will restore our faith in what will probably be our starting net minder next year.

4. Hit somebody. I'm not really sure about the efficacy of this approach, but I've been hollering it for over 45 years and figure now is a bad time to stop. It seems to me, again I have no stats to back it up, we've been much less physical than in the Flames and Canuck's series.

5. Find out who's paying the refs. Before you all told Quenneville to grow up, did anyone look at a replay of the call that got his Irish up? I've said it before and I'll say it again, "Ref, you stink!"

6. I realize this is the wrong approach to be teaching our kids but... with all our Italian brothers in the stand, there has to be someone connected to Familia. Maybe one of their associates should break bread with the referee's, (among a few other things) and discuss some of the finer points of refereeing. I can't help but feel the networks are pining for a Wing/Penguin rematch.

7. Before dressing Martin for game 5, make sure he knows what country he's in. Believe me when I say that every Hawk fan at the U.C. appreciated his intestinal fortitude for trying to play on Sunday. However he looked a bit shaky out there. Even the Wing players avoided hitting him at first. I don't think half a Havlat is worth a whole Jack Skille or Colin Fraser.

8. Win, if nothing else but to make the NBC commentators eat some crow. Coach Q needs to show them the statement by one of the brain trusts in the booth, "More than likely, this will be the last game of the season played at the U.C." Another very agitated friend of mine pointed out, "If Pierre

39

Maguire's so smart, why is he so bald?" Truly, you have to love Hawks fans!

9. Watch the movie Animal House; as Bluto said, "Did we give up when the Germans bombed Pearl Harbor?"

10. Finally, I've coached a few Little League teams that have suffered the ignominy of the slaughter rule. There's not a much lower feeling in the world. However, over the years I've discovered that a milk shake from Dairy Queen is a certain remedy to make the team forget about how bad they played. Coach Q, I know you think I'm nuts, but take the team to DQ today. If they want, let them get the large size.

We'll definitely need some Angels in the Rafters to pull this series out. Regardless of the outcome, what a season it's been. While exceeding our expectations, it's in our human nature to always want more. Despite all the evidence to the contrary I, remain cautiously optimistic at least about tonight's game.

In closing I'm reminded of a cartoon about ice fisherman, truly the last great thinkers of our world. In the scene a Martian space craft is hovering above a lake with several ice fishermen on it. The alien in the space craft calls back to the mother planet and says, "No, there is no intelligent life on this planet." I think anyone picking the Hawks tonight would be lumped in with the ice fishermen, but...

"the ruling passion conquers reason still." The Hawks will be back at the U.C. on Saturday. If I can locate a ticket, I'll expect Chris to buy me a beer!

10/01/09

Real men of genius.

Have you ever sat next to someone at the U.C. who was so inebriated they had problems constructing a coherent sentence? It can be comical, aggravating and somewhat perilous. At the preseason game against the Caps, despite the Hawk management's best attempt to bring back prohibition to Chicago ($7.75 for a Honkers Ale!), we ended up sitting a row behind "Mr. Marriage Scoreboard Proposal Guy". (A close relative of Mr. Roller Cooler, Cooler Rolling Guy. It's got wheels!) One can only hope he's in the bathroom barfing, or the damsel whose hand he seeks shrieks', "NO!", when the proposal is flashed. Yet, we all know love is blind. At this point in their relationship, she probably thinks he's cute when he's had a few to many.

Most of you are probably too young to recall the Andy Griffith show. The moon shining charmer, Ernest T. Bass, came to mind while we kept a wary eye on this over served lad. Somehow, I could just picture the guy saying, "I can heft you Charlene!" Now I have no problem with amorous suitors hefting their girl friends, but please wait for a stop in the action.

What started a near "brew ha-ha" in this section was when Ernest T. decided to stand up for a few moments, with his back to the ice, seemingly forgetting there was a game taking place. Apparently he was contemplating heading out for another beer run. Unfortunately, Jack Skille ripped home a wicked wrist shot while Ernest T. pondered his next move. This aggravated a fan three rows behind us. "Hey you, moron, row 3, 4rth seat from the end, I missed the goal because of you," he bellowed. Bear in mind I'm in between these loving exchanges with my daughter and son – not exactly the best seat in the house. Ernest T. took offense and hollered back, "So, so did I." This may have been his most coherent sentence of the night. It was a notch above yelling, "Yo mama!"

As is so often the case, agitating someone who is two sheets to the wind, only seems to solidify their denseness. Now Ernest T was standing up on purpose in a feeble attempt to preserve his dignity. A fan sitting next to me could only lament. "We just got season tickets in this section. I hope they don't," as he motioned to Ernest T. and his gang. And to think all I have to do is sit next to Sam Fels. Blessings do indeed come in many guises.

The only confrontation I've ever been involved in, took place in the old Stadium parking lot. Dino Ciccarelli had scored on a late minute rush to help the North Stars triumph that night. As we dejectedly filed out into the parking lot, I over heard a Hawk chick saying how much she hated Cissy boy. Unwittingly I said, "You have to admit, he's a pretty good hockey player,"

It elicited a claw like reflex from Cat Woman. In a split second I had three scratches on my cheek. Her boy friend gave me a, "Sorry, I can't control her," type of look as we ended our dialogue. I had a hard time explaining how I received the scratches at work the next few weeks. You can only begin to imagine the theories that were concocted. (Could Cat Woman and Burrows could be related?)

While on the subject of cheeks, I've been pondering the apparent oxymoron of being a Christian and a hockey fan. Turning the other cheek on the one hand and then yelling "kill him," with my next breath, is causing some internal conflict. My kids and I attend a program called Bible Study Fellowship on Monday nights. (I only missed one Monday last year – Game 6 vs. Vancouver; truly, a small slice of heaven on earth.) When it ended, as I approached Taylor's room, I heard quite a commotion. When I poked my head in the door she was extremely agitated, precipitously close to physical violence. "Dad, tell them there wrong. He says the Hawks won't make the playoffs this year!"

He, turned out to be her teacher, who as it turns out has followed the Hawks through some dry seasons. "The Hawks have spent more time in the desert than Moses," he said obviously yanking her chain. Making matters worse, a boy chimed in, "Hockey isn't even a sport. Football, now that's a sport!" Even I began shouting "Blasphemy!" at this point. As we drove home that night, I told Taylor we could be in big trouble if the Hawks drop two in Finland. Instead, we proudly wore are jersey's to last Monday's class.

Perhaps the strangest fan moment I ever witnessed took place in a Hawk-Maple Leaf game. Terry Ruskowski, who seemed to have a perpetual chip upon his shoulder, had been spearing and slashing one of the Leafs for most of the second period. He finally got the reluctant Leaf to drop his gloves. As the dance began, a fan about 5'9", white dress shirt, and clean appearance slid onto the ice to join the fracas. Within seconds, he took a swipe at the Leaf player who had paired off with Ruskowski. Immediately, all the Maple Leaf players who were waltzing with their Hawk partners, tried to acquaint this fan with their razor sharp skates.

Grant Mulvey tried talking some sense to this lunatic, only to have the fan swing at him. This was just one of those moments when mayhem rules the day. Eventually, about ten security guards dragged him into the Hawk penalty box (How apropos!) where they discussed his anti-social behavior. For a few moments, fist and feet were flying. Finally, the now handcuffed

Hawk enforcer jumped straight up. I'm not sure why, but I believe we gave him a standing ovation. One can only speculate whose head hurt more the next morning, this "Real Man of Genius" or Ernest T's.

The ironic part of this episode from Bizzaro World was that there wasn't even a hard check the rest of the game. While none of the players joined the Peace Corps the next day, temporarily, this fan had managed to take the violence out of hockey! The strip teasing Ned Braden, the pusillanimous pacifist of the Chiefs, had nothing on this guy.

Hockey, don't you just love it! I suspect if you're still reading this meandering recollection, you probably found away to watch the game last Friday morning in Helsinki. Hawkhead's, other than the ludicrous beer prices, you have to be optimistic after our first two games. It turns out most of the customers who I talked to Friday weren't even aware the season was starting. When I told them I had joined a fantasy hockey league, they began to have reservations of placing orders with me.

The foray into the Fantasy League will no doubt increase my hockey knowledge. Perhaps some of my player observations will begin to make sense. In what I think will turn out to be one of my more brilliant moves, I added Buffy to my fantasy team. Look for a big year from the right winger formerly known as "Laissez-faire." Dustin, you have the ability to make me look like a genius – don't blow it!

Other observations – Cam is starting to "bark like a dog" in front of his crease. His confidence seems to have been raised a notch or two - ditto Hjalmarsson on the burgeoning confidence. Niklas is Soupy's back door man, allowing Campbell to try to play the role of a guy who wore #4 for Boston. (Bobby Orr was a stone cold hockey freak of nature – never saw anyone like him.) I know it's a little early to start with the DK Admiration Society angle, but from all appearances the Duncster appears to have regained the half step he lost after getting conked last year. Seabs is starting to enjoy hurting people. In short, our toddling defensemen appear to be entering adulthood.

Madden is as good a two way hockey player as we have. That is saying a lot with Toews and Bolland on your team. I like Huet between the pipes. Niemi, looks to be an adequate back up. Did you notice the save he invented in the 3rd period last Saturday – "The Luge Save." Basically you lay perpendicular to the goal line, scissor you legs closed, and lift your head to get a glimpse of the grinders attempting to amputate your legs.

Well, I could go on and on with my giddy exuberance. What I guess I'm trying to say is, wouldn't it be great to see some Hawks "hefting" that

30# cup next June in the U.C.? Also, I can't recall if I've mentioned it, has anyone noticed the ridiculous beer prices? Where have you gone Al Capone, the 300 section turns it thirsty eyes to you..." I'll bet Cat Woman has a purse with a trap door – let the smuggling begin!

"Let me woo you with my ways Charlene."

10/15/09

The Tortoise and the Hare; a night to remember.

Aesop's Fable's, after centuries of bed time story telling, are still poignant and timeless. Perhaps more than any other explanation of what transpired at the U.C. last Monday, the classic fable of the Tortoise and the Hare holds the key. Although, it is highly probable that some things just defy an explanation. In an attempt to describe what I saw with my own eyes, I was left pondering the headline of the Committed Indian. The headline read, "And this is my other brother Darryl." Sam Fels title reminded me of another situation that just didn't seem to flow like it should have. It involved complete strangers, golf and the Darryl brothers from the Bob Newhart show.

My brother and I joined up with a twosome in front of us do to a logjam on the 15th hole at Deer Creek one day. I was having a fortunate round so I was, temporarily at least, in a jovial mood. Trying to strike up a conversation, I thought I'd use a little humor to break the ice. While introducing myself to the hackers that joined us, I said "Hi, my names Darryl and this is my brother Darryl," quite amused by my cleverness. Shock overtook me when he replied, "My name is Darryl."

As I began to dig a hole that would get progressively deeper, I nervously laughed and said, "You're kidding, right?" After he convinced me he was indeed Darryl, I tried to explain my humor. I asked Darryl if he had ever watched the Bob Newhart show. The hole I was digging was approaching Grand Canyon type proportions when he answered, "No." Then I tried to explain the show and its characters, to no avail. I think I triple bogeyed number 16, as the lake on the right side collected yet another of my wayward drives on that diabolical hole.

My point is, what are the odds of that embarrassing exchange taking place, or me recalling it 20 years later do to a headline in the Committed Indian? The hole I dug that day paled in comparison to the one the Hawks found themselves in against the Flames.

Who would have thought this bizarre circumstance would help us make sense out of what turned out to be the greatest comeback in Hawks history. There are some situations in life that can only be explained by Rod Sterling's unsettling voice "You have just entered the Twilight Zone." As the Blackhawk's skated in what appeared to be a Black Hole, it actually went from aggravating to almost comical. The blonde bimbo's that shoot the puck in between periods could have scored on us, and would have been a lot more enjoyable to watch.

The Flames came out smoking for the first 12 min., as we fans became intimately connected with the phrase, "Shock and Awe." It appeared the Flames had downed two bottles each of one of those energy drinks with 5000 grams of caffeine and sugar in them. The Hawks were not a half step slow getting to loose pucks, it appeared they were skating on double rudders. Those eerie 12 minutes appeared to be an uncut, pre-showing of the Calgary Chain Saw Massacre.

After the shavings had settled, the stupefied U.C. crowd thought of ways to keep themselves amused. Derisively cheering our goalies seemed to be the fan consensus. As I watched the Ice Crew scrape up the shavings I thought aloud, "I wonder what the qualifications are to become Ice Crew members?" My friend Joel, without hesitation said, "Well, you have to be able to skate first of all..." This made me laugh so hard I almost forgot about the score. Down 5-0 the Over/Under bet on how many fans would be left after the second period, was 2,000. Positive Mental Attitude had, as Elvis, left the building.

Then, the increasingly popular John Madden pounced on a loose puck, exposing the first chink in Kiprusoff's armor. It proved to be the ember that ignited a roaring comeback. With two minutes to go in the first, I headed to the washroom to beat the crowds that would no doubt be vomiting in between periods. When I returned, I stopped by and sat on the stairs by RoseLee and Earl to ask them if they could recall anything like it in their 6 decades of following the red shirts. Heading back to my seat I told them, "Who knows, we may just see the greatest comeback in Blackhawk history!" RoseLee's smile seemed to indicate she was on board with the notion, despite our dismal chances. Earl turned his I-pod up to drown out my incoherent babbling!

What happened next is recorded on my Blackberry. Step by step, inch by inch, slowly the Hawks crept back into the contest. When the Hawks made it 5-2, I immediately texted my wife and daughter who had turned off the radio by this time in utter disgust. At 8:16 they received this text, "5-2 Kaner- greatest comeback ever." At 8:27 I texted "5-3 Buff – greatest comeback ever." At 8:28 the text simply read "5-4" as I high fived nearly every hand in sec 101! Finally, at 9:05 I texted the incredible news, "5-5, Sharpie – Who called it!" the text recorded at 9:32 was almost anticlimactic, "Hawks Win!" The air in the U.C. that was so putrid 2 hours earlier could now only be described as rarefied.

While I'm at a loss of words to explain the "Outer Limits," (Do not attempt to adjust the dials on your TV), portion of the game, what happened in the next 48:29 was elementary my dear Watson. It didn't start with adjusting the knobs on your TV; it began with some bone jarring checks. When all else fails, HIT SOMEBODY! The Hawks decided they were going to go down swinging.

I think it was Buff who tried to extinguish a Flame by knocking him through the Plexiglas. Generally speaking, it's hard to beat someone to the puck when you're sitting on your duff! I appreciated Colin Fraser's attempt to hit one of Calgary's Jolly Green Giants, even though Colin went "timber!" It's the thought that counts. The highly intelligent #16 car for the Hawks appeared to be in a demolition derby in Jackson Mississippi on a Saturday night. Not many players in the league outwork Ladd.

I must make it clear that while I don't condone fisticuffs on the ice, they do indeed serve a purpose at times. In fact I have to admit, I secretly enjoy some of the knuckleheads on the opposition getting pounded. Now some of you may have scored the bout between Iginla and Brouwer differently than me. I believe Troy emerged victorious.

Apparently taking a page from the "Burr-dog" playbook, Brouwer repeatedly head butted Jarome's fist. It was an ingenious strategy that affected Iginla's stick handling ability the rest of the game! Now this is just me thinking, but I thought Toews should have dropped the gloves when that Flaming defenseman punched him for no apparent reason. I don't want anyone to think I'm light in the loafers, but Toews has a physique that resembles the Greek God, Apollo. "Bumping it up Jack," with the moron who hit him may have been just what Jonny boy needed to jump start his game, and the team. By the way, for those of you who think Toews is struggling, check out his team high +4 plus/minus rating.

Although a lot of you probably missed it because you hate Sopel as much as Huet, the conversation in front of the Hawk bench between Sope's and Killer Carlson, err I mean McGratten, is one of those intangibles that never show up on the score sheet. Although I'm afraid it would not have produced a positive outcome, I had to admire Sopel apparently trying to adjust Killer Carlson's tie, while trying to get him to renounce his evil ways! I'm pretty sure Sopel was saying, "Repent sinner."

On to a touché subject; Cristobal Huet. Anyone who blames Huet for Boyd's or Igilna's goal should be drawn and quartered. Again I'll defer to RoseLee who has seen some pretty good goaltenders over the last 57 years. "There wasn't a red shirt near the goal when those first three shots were fired. I regret that after the fantastic outing he had during the shootout the game before that the crowd so quickly turned on him."

Brent Seabrook came as close to anybody in describing the weird events of the infamous 12 minutes in period one, **"WE"** played like crap." If you're going to blame Cristobal for that outing, you may as well blame him for the debacle at Waterloo. (On a side note: Cristobal – stop closing your eyes when the puck is fired at you!) As I recall many of you were hoping to see Habby's head in the guillotine last year.

Was it just me, or does Kaner have eyes in the back of his head. His performance reminded me of that little devil on Detroit named Datsyuk. It was like the puck was magnetic and his stick was the North Pole. His feather touch pass to Buffy was a sight for sore eyes. I read Chris Block's column in the C.I. last Monday, and something just dawned on me. When someone like Chris puts you in a category with the players he names, it makes you realize just what we have in this player who was once labeled "the best player in a weak draft." I do believe John McDonough missed a golden opportunity when he didn't have Patrick arrive in a cab on red carpet night!

Two last observations; Hjarlmasson is beginning to resemble Duncan Keith on defense. He prances around like a figure skater trying to escape from Tonya Harding. Even with his partner abandoning his post while leading the rushes, Niklas is a +2. Also, I think we need to put Keith on the point on power plays. He's my main defensive dog and I desperately need his P.P points for my fantasy team.

In conclusion, I received a call from my credit card company investigating the possibility of fraudulent usage on Tuesday morning. We got excited during the Hawks comeback and I purchased several rounds of Honkers Ale. While I didn't max the card out, the cost of a round of 4 beers apparently was enough to trigger an investigation! We're in a damn recession, lower the prices. Also turn the horn down about 50 decibels.

By the way, if you still have your copy of Monday's Committed Indian, look at Sam's last sentence on page one; "It should be a fun one." We may have a prophet in our midst.

For all who attended, it was a night to remember. As Dana Garvey put it in the classic movie, MASTER OF DISGUISE, "turtle!"

Shedding light on going into dark corners...

It's no secret that hockey games are won in that treacherous area of the rink known as the corner. The corners, like shootouts, are not for the faint of heart. I recall playing rat hockey many moons ago with some friends from the Beverly area, many of whom attended Mt. Carmel High School. Needless to say, I was a bit out of my league. One of my friends and I headed into the corner with a full head of steam to chase down the rubber. It needs to be pointed out that Tom had about 100 pounds on me. Not to worry I thought, surely a gazelle like me would have no problem beating a water buffalo like Tom to the puck.

As I shifted into 4rth gear, approaching warp speed, I nervously looked over my shoulder to see if I had left Tom in my shavings. What I saw has left me with recurring nightmares some 30 years later. Tom, who appeared to be in 2nd or 3rd gear, was smiling at me! Not only that, he did this weird thing with his eyebrows, which appeared to be twitching up and down. Discretion became the better part of valor I must reluctantly admit, with Tom easily emerging with the puck. Or maybe it was the coach was screaming for me to come off on a line change..., yeah that's what it was.

Another battle I lose quite frequently is one concerning house cleaning. Nathalie occasionally admonishes me for doing a superficial job when vacuuming. Keeping up with our 105 # Akita and his daily deposit of fur, is a never ending task. I'm pretty good at the heavy traffic areas, although no one will ever confuse me with a detail man. The area beneath the chairs, couches and yes the dreaded corners, tend to get only sporadic attention.

Last Saturday I worked a bit more assiduously trying to get to those hard to reach areas. While on my hands and knees, I noticed a little piece of what appeared to be a ticket stub sticking out from under this huge cabinet in our mudroom. When I pulled it out, it brought a smile to my face. It was a ticket stub from a game on Jan. 17, 2006 against the Islanders. We lost 2-1 that night.

What really threw me for a loop as I gazed at the ticket was the price for a seat in the 100 section. The seat which now costs $115, sold for $67.50 in the 05-06 season. Our record was a stellar 26-43-13, with Habby minding the nets for us. (Actually Craig Anderson saw a little time between the pipes also.) At this point in the season, many season ticket holders were questioning the return on their season ticket investment.

Fast forward to the 07/08 season; on a dollar vs. value basis, I don't think a ticket deal like that will ever materialize in my life time again. $10 to sit in the boonies and watch professional hockey, knowing you had two of the brightest stars in the NHL! C'mon tell me that don't beat the hell out of paying $8 to see Shrek 3. That season, (even though we narrowly missed making the playoffs because Toews decided to take a midseason vacation for about 15 games), will be one of my all time favorites. Lamentably, excellence does come with a steep price tag.

The 05-06 season did have a few bright spots though. Two young defensemen, Keith and Seabs, had a lot of ice time in their rookie year. Cam Barker put on the Indian head for the first time, as did the Buffy. I recall asking one of the two guys who sit in row 15, "Who's that and where did he come from?", as I delightedly watch Dustin go coast to coast. I recall he told me he wasn't sure and then said it doesn't matter, "We stink."

Sharp, Calder, Borque and Bell were also on that team, so there did appear to be some light at the end of the long, dark tunnel. Mark Bell's poster adorned the wall in my daughter's bedroom until she saw Toews play. It appeared perhaps are biggest weakness that year was at the center position. I doubt that any of the following names will ever be hanging in the rafters – Holmqvist, Cullen, Brown or St. Pierre.

One thing I'm quite sure of, when we play teams in the Central division, we'd better be ready to head for the corners. When the group that I share season tickets with divide the games up, it always seems we shy away from the Blue Jacket, Predator and to some extent, Blues games. Yet, I've come to realize that whenever one of those teams step onto our ice, we better be packing! There almost always highly entertaining games. I'm not sure how the Pred's do it, but they continue to be a proverbial pain in the butt. When's the last time you've seen us blow out the Blue Jackets. The Blues seem to drop the gloves against us more than any team we face. They just do not play well with others.

Last Tuesday's game against the Jackets appeared that it was going to have to be settled by a coin toss. While we didn't quite have to resort to it, I saw Haviland telling Niemi to take off his goalie pads when we reached the tenth shooter! After playing some very good teams on the West Coast, I think a lot of us thought Columbus would give us a chance to catch our breath; wrong.

In my mind, Huet had a solid game before the shoot out. One area that has seemed to be a weakness for our flopping Frenchman has been, as Sam described it, his slothful glove hand. It was smoking on Tuesday. I believe the best save of the day was on a wicked, partially screened wrist shot off the stick of Nash late in the third period. As he skated from North to South in our zone, with our defensemen paying him way too much respect, he ripped a shot that appeared to be heading just inside the post. Cristobal stabbed it like Robert Mitchum grabbing the fly in the movie *The Magnificent Seven*. I dare ya, try and catch a fly with your hand someday. (And then try to figure out what to do with it!)

I "think" that I don't like shootouts. It seems like a cheap way to decide a game and tends to cause anxiety attacks. I do have to admit, after the 22nd shot in Tuesday night's affair, I'm glad we came away with the W. Huet was huge, pumping his fists with increasing enthusiasm as one Blue Jacket after another was repelled. Mason was also outstanding, coming up a brick short in the wall he tried to construct. Although our goalie situation appears to be quite solid un momente, I fear unless we win the Cup, the Huet haters, filled with angst, will blame him. Just a little pressure to contend with! Drink more red wine, #39.

Versteeg actually had a chance to finish the game about half way through the shootout. He deked Mason out of his jockstrap, before deciding to go through a non existent 5 hole. This wouldn't have been so bad if 60% of a wide open net wasn't pleading for a deposit. Verstud's short handed goal will most likely take the place of Toews's goal against the Avalanche on the highlight reel. Jonny got nothing on Steegs.

Which brings us to Laddie; I think Sam Fels needs to work on a top 10 reasons Andrew decided to attack the net without the puck, when he dumped it towards the corner;

1. Sneak attack.

2. Playing with Mason's mind

3. Lulling Mason into a false sense of security

4. Wanted a challenge after depositing the game winner in the shoot out vs. Colorado.

5. Versteeg double dog dared him

6. Heard Mason's weakness is severe angles from the right dash board.

7. He was thinking wrap around. Or his trade mark dump and chase.

8. Thought he'd physically plow into the net like Sharpie does.

9. Tried to skate with his head up, stick handle and chew bubble gum at the same time.

10. He thought his imaginary friend would pass it back to him.

Whatever his thought process, or lack thereof, he deserved to go through a spanking machine in the locker room. While I appreciate how hard Ladd goes into the dark corners, he might rethink this strategy if Quenneville is crazy enough to call his number again in a shootout.

Oh, by the way. A guy named Hossa had two assists and a shootout goal. We no longer stink!

12/26/09

And then the fight started.

The book *Spiritual Sayings*, by Lebanese author Kahlil Gibran, has me pondering the Hawk salary cap dilemma. The book is packed with wisdom. I realize wisdom and hockey fans are not words generally associated with each other. I'll be the first to admit, his thoughts are not my thoughts. Most likely I misinterpret a lot of what he writes, however there is one saying that I'll never forget and think I have a basic understanding of;

"Love knows not its depth until the hour of separation."

The ebullient joy accompanied by the signing of the Blackhawk holy trinity to extended contracts, is being quickly displaced by the realization that more than one very popular Hawk will be soon exiting, stage left, most likely before the season ends. That scourge, or should I say Scrooge at this time of year, known as the Salary Cap looms like a Christmas fruitcake. The most likely suspects will probably be those making between 2 and 4 million clams. Can you imagine any of the following wearing a Predator, Blues or Blue Jacket sweater before season end – Sharp, Steegs, Buffy, Barks, Sopel, Madden or Bolland. The Blues sure could use a couple of our defensemen.

Obviously you could add Huet or Campbell to that list. With their onerous, long term contracts, it's not very likely they will be skating on a different pond any time soon. Please don't get me wrong, despite the incessant lynch mobs scattered throughout the U.C. calling for their immediate resignation, I actually believe Cristobal and Brian are money players. Anyone out there particularly fond of breaking up the Campbell/Hjarlmarrson tandem at the moment – I didn't think so. Despite the final tally, I thought the Blues played ok on Wednesday. I'd add Perron, Backes or Oshie to my team in a heart beat. In my mind, the difference in Wednesday's tussle was our defense.

Huet is far better than most of his detractors will admit, quietly compiling a 2.10 GAA that is fourth in the league! I was at a local saloon watching the Sabre's game last Friday when a friend asked me, "Do you like Huet?" When I said, "Indubitably so," he gave me a puzzled look and finally said, "So does that mean yes or no." And Then The Fight Started...

After five minutes of futile debating I was told in so many words, "We should have kept Habby. Huet will never take us to the Cup." Now let me think a moment, how many goalies got to the Cup last year? Oh that's right just two, Fleury and Osgood. And, of course, Osgood sucks because he didn't win it. I seem to recall that impregnable fortress otherwise known as Luongo yielding 7 goals in the Conference Semi-Finals last year.

Actually, there must have been a Blue Moon out last Wednesday when the Hawks sent "Spanky and the Gang" back to St. Louis with their tails between their legs. (Nice team photo Sam!) With less than a minute in the game, I swore I heard the U.C. crowd chanting HU-ET, HU-ET, HU-ET! This strange phenomenon occurred moments after Cristobal flattened Jannsen for illegally parking in his crease. Huet finally had enough of his stench shouting, "Time expired" as he labeled the Blues goon with a wicked cross check to the back. Billy Smith would have been proud of him! If Huet wants to get a good deal of the fans in the U.C. on his side, swinging his goalie stick like a tomahawk will do it. By the way, is it just me or does it appear Huet is smiling all the time through his goalie mask? Maybe he's just crazy.

Well since it doesn't appear Huet or Campbell will be doing triple axles in another rink anytime soon, that brings us back to the Magnificent Seven. Sopel, who many thought would be missed as much as a canker sore, has been outstanding in our zone. He's blocked so many shots, it appears we have two net minders on the ice at times. Plus he adds that intangible that can't be taught – he looks real scary. I'm thinking he has a little Transylvanian blood in his hereditary line.

There aren't too many teams in the league that would not improve if Sharpie was added to their roster. No doubt, all the damsels at the U.C. would get their panties in a thither if the Hawks traded him. I'm afraid my wife would quit following the Hawks. Madden has been a great pickup and has been a huge factor in the winning equation. Winning face offs, while not a glamorous part of hockey, wins games. You have to love how John hustles back into our zone. Lunch bucket players are somewhat idolized in Chi-town.

Versteeg adds so much to the team, including that rare combination of speed, ability and goofiness. In fact, that's a pretty good description of #32 – "a goofy, Usain Bolt." By the way, Toews's latest highlight reel goal got nothing on Steeger's goal vs. Columbus. Bolland and his aching sacroiliac are sorely missed, but he appears to be safe for the moment. Byfuglien, is really gaining a foothold with the fans who miss Ruutu's atomic hits.

Ted Nugent has a great song called Great White Buffalo that has some intense guitar licks in it. If Dustin always played with the intensity that the Motor City Madman does, his autograph line would be as long as Kanes. While not as long as Kane's line, the Buffster's autograph line was almost as long as Hossa'a at the Season Ticket Holders Holiday Party. Cam Barker appeared to be visually shaken when looking at the length of Byfuglien's line.

Barkey, in my opinion, just keeps improving every year. (Actually I'd like to see him and Campbell paired more together on the power play.) He may be able to fill Campbell's spot eventually if Brian should be acquired by another team. By the way is it just me, or is anyone else noticing Cameron throwing his weight around more this year. I've definitely seen him clobber a couple people.

Cam's biggest draw back is he needs to get rid of that boyish look and start resembling Sopel more. Generally speaking, hockey players are not supposed to look like pretty boys. This brings me to a short anecdote about my daughter Taylor.

Taylor is the antipode of the word "Morning Person." Her language before ten in the morning is reduced to grunts and unintelligible mumblings. While driving to school on Monday morning I tried to strike up a conversation. Nothing worked until I said, "Hey Tay, Kaner got stitches and a black eye last night. Now he's going to look like a hockey player!" This brought a smile to her face from ear to ear. Again, hockey players should never be spending a lot of time standing in front of a mirror.

While on the subject of ugly mugs, if you're looking for a sleeper on the Hawks, Troy Brouwer is a sagacious choice in your Fantasy Leagues. He plays a lot of Sunday and Friday games where you can plug him in when not many teams are playing. If he can remember to keep his stick on the ice, Kaner should be able to deflect a lot of shots off it into the goal.

Oh well, for those of us who have followed the incredible resurgence in Blackhawk hockey that really kicked into gear in the 07/08 season, some painful decisions will have to be made. I don't have time to research the stats, but looking at the Predators line up, there has to be some salary cap room. St. Louis and Columbus both could add a Hawk or two and become a better team. Unfortunately, I believe two out of the 7 players I've mentioned will be gone before year end.

The thought of getting a second or third round draft pick for any of those players is not a pleasant one. RoseLee's statement last year that "it's hard to distinguish between love and loyalty" comes to mind when we think of losing one of these warriors. Hockey fans appreciate the hard play and doggedly determined efforts of players. In a weird sort of way, they become like family.

Lamentably, in the midst of this long awaited season, the dark cloud that follows Eeyore around continues to linger. Maybe if each player gave up 10% of their contract. (Fat chance, that family thing only goes so far; Cousin Eddy comes to mind.) Think about it, we could have a dynasty that would overcome the Tribunes propensity to relegate the Blackhawks to page 6 or 8 of the sports section. All the Hawk players could open up restaurants and perhaps pick up some of Tiger's endorsements.

Until the axe falls however, let's enjoy those warriors we've exhorted on the last two years. I'm reminded of that Jackson Browne song, "Stay, just a little bit longer..."

One last saying from Kahlil Gibran:

At ebb tide I wrote
A line upon the sand
And gave it all my heart
And all my soul.
At flood tide I returned
To read what I had inscribed
And found my ignorance upon the shore

In the shifting sands of Blackhawk hockey, it's quite apparent a few names will vanish with the close of the 09/10 season. However, the hour of separation is not upon us yet.

Lets go out with a BANG!

12/29/09

Better Living Through Chemisrty

For the past two and a half seasons, without overstating the obvious, the Hawks have concocted a team chemistry that would rival Watson and Crick's discovery of the double helix. Emerging from the primordial soup of mediocre hockey, the Hawks have mutated into one of the best teams I've ever followed in Chi-town. Darwin's theory of evolution notes that 99% of mutations are considered deleterious. However, it seems with every mutation, heretofore known as adding one knucklehead and subtracting another, the Hawks have increased their chances of survival. Coach Q's latest line formulations should win him the Nobel Prize in Chemistry.

Start with Kane, Toews (the Hawks new muscle?) and Brou-dog, or as I like to refer to him, "Digging Dog." I recall the first time I saw Toews and Kane play, against the Avalanche in early 2007, noting immediately that we had something special under the Bunsen burner. There's some sort of weird cosmic thing going on with those two. Think ying and yang, Batman and Robin or Rocky and Bullwinkle. As different as a proton and an electron in individual qualities, their synergistic effect is a sight to behold. Adding Brouwer to the line, (the catalyst?), is proving to be an alchemists dream. Both Toews and Brouwer tend to open up the ice for our "Little Big Man."

On the post game show, Kaner was asked if he mentioned anything to Brouwer about missing the wide open net. Kane replied that he asked Troy, "Hey Brouw, what happened on that shot?" Troy told Kane that he didn't see the puck through all the traffic.. Patrick replied "Man, just keep your stick on the ice and I'll deflect it off your stick next time!" Brouwer threatened to stop screening for Kane if he continued to pursue this line of questioning. Apparently Toews was oblivious to this chemistry building banter, as he scoured the ice for his next dance partner. You could almost see him thinking, "I'll bet I could I could open a can of whoop-ass on Havlat." Let the rest of the league take note, Chief War Paint is on the prowl.

Our current second line of Sharp, Hossa and Ladd is firing on all eight. Let me ask you something; was the two month delay for Marian to join the team worth the wait? I was told after we acquired the oft traded journeyman, (Yuk, yuk), that he was a top ten player. Now I'm beginning to see why. Hossa has that rare ability, much like Kane and Datsyuk, to appear to play keep away with the puck. Ladd might be the hardest working corner guy on the team. Rumor has it, when he doesn't dump the puck into the corners on shootout attempts, he's a threat offensively. He was not only the friendliest Hawk at the Holiday Party at Navy Pier, he appears to be the brightest.

Sharpie, whose name unfortunately continues to surface in the process of jettisoning salaries, has been one of the basic elements in rejuvenating Blackhawk hockey. He went into a minor slump a few weeks back which prompted RoseLee to observe, "I think he might be trying to tone down his game so he doesn't look to attractive to other teams." Fat chance if he stays on this line. I feel comfortable going out on a limb to say Patrick could end up around 35 goals this year, not counting the times he physically plows into the net himself. Did anyone else notice Brouwer trying this approach on Harding last Tuesday at the end of the game? Who can deny our second line (?) is strong, talented and dangerous.

It doesn't get much easier for our opponents when Buff, Steeger and Madden jump over the boards. Versteeg resembles a free radical, possessing an indomitable spirit as he buzzes around the ice in search of the puck or whatever. He just seems happy to be out there skating his butt off. Despite being told over and ever and over again that you can't stick handle past 5 opponents, it will never stop Kris from trying. The Buffster has appeared to be an Apollo Ohno at times this year. He seems to have a 5th or 6th gear, a quantum leap if you will, that has caught more than one opponent off guard. The way he's been crushing opponents lately, it would appear he is a huge proponent of "The Big Bang Theory." I can't help but think a lot of teams would like the 6'4", 260 pound thumper.

The picture Sam Fels posted on the website of Madden celebrating the goal against the Nashville Pests, was a classic. He looked like a 10 year old kid, not the imperturbable 36 year old defensive specialist added to shadow the opponent's top centers. Toews should study that picture to learn how to celebrate goals. Sometimes when Jonathan scores his celebration seems to say, "So what, that's what I'm paid to do. Now who can I go postal on next."

I read on one of the blogs that Madden and Toews will not let this team lose. Someone pointed out Toews would skate 60 minutes/game if necessary. Madden might not have a C on his sweater but it's embedded in his heart.

Fourth lines tend to take on a life of their own. Our opponents would be wise not to underestimate the Hawks fourth line. I'm not sure if its gay, but this line does have pride. Colin Fraser is the epitome of a stick your nose in it hockey player. Ben Eager, currently number two behind Toews in the tough guy category, has considerable offensive abilities. His play may be a bit hindered this year without his body guard, Burr-dog, covering his back. Big Ben reminds me of the kid at school that used to try extorting my lunch money. I never did find the location of the elevator.

Kopecky struggled a bit to fit in initially, but generally speaking is better liked than Huet. The last few games, there does seem to be a good chemistry emerging with this trio. Lets call it Chemistry 101. They've been getting a lot more time in the third period lately with the lopsided nature of the last few games. Not a bad idea to rest our million dollar babies for the playoff wars.

Of course, as the sagacious Sam Fels noted, Coach Q changes his lines more than David Byrne of the Talking Heads changes hairstyles. Hopefully, he'll let these lines stay together for awhile. Chemistry is everything when it comes to team play. It's one of the reasons I think the unsubstantiated rumors floating around about Kovalchuk would prove to be a disaster. Trading players like Barker and Versteeg to add a player who would be with us for 2 – 3 months? As Marquette basketball Coach Al McGuire pointed out so many moons ago, "You dance with the girl you brought to the prom."

While on the subject of dancing, I now know why Captain Marvel is reluctant to drop the gloves. Jonathan made former Hawk enforcer Keith Magnuson look like the heavy weight champion of the world. Help me out here, but didn't Toews's tussle with Backes resemble a bad version of The Electric Slide? I think Jonny needs to spend some quality time with Burrish and Eager. Maybe spend a little time with Kaner and his cousin in the back of a cab.

Before the season is over, I may have to resort to violence when defending our embattled net minder, Cristobal Huet. I've come to the conclusion that his detractors would rather see him fail, than the Hawks win. I was watching the Wild game with about 8 other people at a friend's house on Tuesday. Towards the end of the game Huet made a great point blank save, and then another one on the rebound. I won't mention any names, but Donny almost stood up to cheer when the rebound appeared to be heading for the twine. When Huet made the save, he actually went, "Darn."

The Hawks currently have the best record in the NHL. Who knows, perhaps we might be undefeated if only we could pick up a real goalie. Please!! Actually my son Greg made a poignant observation concerning Huets bad luck at times this year – change back to # 38. Think about it Cristobal.

Finally, while on the subject of Crystal Balls, if one more analyst says, the Hawk/Devil, Hawk/Sabres, Hawk/Penguins or Hawk/Bruins could be a preview of the Stanley Cup final I'm going to pull my hair out. Is anybody really relishing playing a healthy Red Wing team that squeaks into the playoffs in the first round? It takes 20 committed players, fortuitous bounces, lady luck, hot goal tending and above all – great team chemistry. As Huet critics might point out, 4 out of 5 ain't bad.

02/15/10

My Goal . . .

Goals are a great thing to strive for in life. (They really come in handy for hockey players.) Think of all the goals we accomplish in a life time. Walking, talking, reading, playing well with others (Eager needs to work on this one a little), graduating from Catholic grade school with less than 4 broken knuckles, staying married for 50 years, keeping your daughter out of the back seat of limo's, receiving an organ transplant even if it did mean you'd forever have a little "Blues" blood in you, only scratch the surface. If you're really ambitious, you may even try to reduce the National deficit, one that requires us to pay $684 million per day in interest. And you thought Huet was a profligate use of money!

Certainly for those of us numbered among the Blackhawk Nation, we have that elusive goal of seeing Lord Stanley's Cup hoisted towards the rafters. Ah, to dream the impossible dream. In order to achieve that goal, it will require that many smaller goals be accomplished along the way. That goal is only met after lesser goals of repairing wounded warriors, winning face offs and the battles in the corner. It would help considerably if we stopped the opposition from loitering in front of the net. (The front of the net is perhaps the Hawks biggest concern at the moment.) Little goals like working every second of every shift, or taking a bone jarring hit to get the puck the hell out of our zone. (Jordan Hendry comes to mind.)

As I sat at a friend's house watching a game recently, I turned to those present and joyfully stated, "I love watching hockey!" with an ear to ear smile on my face. (Ok, I admit it. We were winning at the time.) It was at that moment the angst and incessant worry about the Big Goal abated. No more chewing finger nails, no more worrying about Huet's latest alleged soft goal, no more worrying about getting swept by Detroit in the first round of the playoffs. I decided to just sit back and savor each moment of this magical season, one game at a time. You see, I'm beginning to realize its not so much the end result – it's the dance.

Garth Brooks wrote the following song that contains some sage advice for us worry warts;

And now I'm glad I didn't know
The way it all would end the way it
all would go
Our lives are better left to chance I
could have missed the pain

But I'd of had to miss the dance

Increasingly, in my simple mind, it's not so much the end result; it's the effort of the moment, the dance. While I seldom disagree with Sam Fels insight, his statement that "Frankly, a lot of these games feel like they don't mean all that much," is not true. Try as you may, it would be hard to convince me that 21,800 fans weren't sitting on the edge of their seat when Huet abandoned the outpost with a minute left against the surging Blues. All that to say, **"My Goal," - Savor every precious moment of this season.**

One moment that really irked me was not getting a Fu Man 2 bobble head, despite arriving an hour before game time. Taylor cried for 3 days last year when she didn't get the Tazer Bobble Head. After that game I recall asking about 10 middle aged men if I could buy their false idol figurine, (Clearly a violation of the second commandment.), only to hear some of the lamest excuses ever construed; "I need to give it to my son," (light in the loafers) "I need it to complete my collection," (gay boy) "I'm going to sell it on e bay," (dancing queen).

Please except my apologies if I appear to be disparaging the Hawk's gay fans. I know there's a couple Ned Braden's listed among the Hawk faithful. To their credit, I realize 99.9% of those happy blades in the stands would not consider a Bobble Head fine art. Do any of you grown men realize how gay you look carrying out the Bobble Head box? Give the damn thing to the kids! **"My Goal," Camp out in front of gate 3 on March 4th to be the first in line for the Tazer Bobble Head give away on the 5th.**

By the way, despite being Co-Founder and President of the Duncan Keith Admiration Society, even I must admit the Duncster played like a Bobble Head at times against the Blues. Maybe it was the pressure of knowing 10,000 grown men were holding your Bobble Head that affected his play. Never one to dwell on the negative, I'd like to mention one of the greatest games ever played by a Hawks defenseman. If Troy Brouwer was the highlight of the recent 8 game road trip, Keith was the MVP of the Shark slaying in San Jose. Actually Duncan resembles the great white shark hunter, Quint, in the movie Jaws. In that game, #2 on the Hawks was a man among Bobble Heads. He skated around as if he heard a constant recording of The Flight of the Bumble Bee in his helmet. **"My Goal," – try not to root for Keith and Seabs when they face Team USA in the finals in Vancouver.**

If there is a weakness in our Norris Trophy candidate, it could be clearing out the front of our net. In fact as a whole, it seems to be an area of concern for our D-men. While I realize many of the amateur goalies, holding their big fat Bobble Heads in the stands, could easily stop a 90mph redirect, Huet has a little problem with them. (Not to mention almost every other masked man in the league.) **"My Goal," – convince our D-men that the area in front of Huet's crease is OUR TURF! If need be we will bring in the Bloods and Crips to defend it. "Hit Somebody!"**

While on the subject of "hitting" on someone, I must say I had an uneasy feeling the Hawks would make the headlines for some reason other than their exploits on the ice during their road trip. Somewhere along the line, woman and booze would enter the Limo, err, I mean picture. Somewhere along the line those Vancouver damsels must have heard the 3 Musketeers had a bulging wallet, among other things. How else could 3 of the homeliest Hawks get them to go for a ride? Maybe Coach Q should get them the road racing set the Hansen brothers used to while away their time in between games. **"My Goal," – keep Kaner out of the back seats of motorized vehicles.**

When Taylor and I dejectedly drove home after the Blues loss, we turned on the post game show hosted by Judd Sirott. I like listening to Judd and his analysis, although he should probably do a better job of screening some of the, there's just no other way to put it, morons who call in to give their myopic views. I thought Judd was going to lose it the other night when a fan called in and said, "I used to be a Hawk fan in the 80's. I'm one of the ones McDonough has brought back. I pay good money for my seat and they need to get rid of Huet." (And here I thought it was players like Toews, Kane and Keith who brought back the fans – my bad.)

As Judd kept asking the erstwhile fan, which of the goals Huet gave up was soft, I believe he finally realized it was like Sarah Palin debating Bill Ayers. Actually, one of the guys who splits season tickets with me is a Huet hater. I thought he was going to attack me the other night when I tried to defend Heut's gross ineptitude. "Pew Wee goalies are better than Huet!" he finally exclaimed with bulging carotid arteries and flaming nostrils. "He's the worst goalie I've ever seen." **"My Goal," - patiently, in a non-confrontational way, try to make The Man from France haters realize he's not "the worst goalie ever."**

When I was in grade school I read a book about a French speaking hockey player who was ostracized and tormented by the English speaking players on his team. (A little like the Stan Mikita story.) They derisively called him Frenchy, doing everything possible to make him quit. To make a long story short, the book ends with him scoring the winning goal in the championship! I believe he even wins the damsel of his desire – although there was no mention of any Limo. **"My Goal," – watching Cristobal hoist the cup while wearing the Indian Head on his chest.**

Is it just me, or is this season starting to slip away from us? As the Olympics approach, who can't help reflect back on that "Miracle" in 1980. My brother said it best, describing the wild on ice celebration after the USA upset Russia – "It was the ultimate hockey war dance." **"My Goal," – prepare for that magical moment in June by watching re-runs of Soul-Train. It's all about the dance.**

3/23/10

Nacho Macho Man

"Hey Bob, we need to take the violence out of hockey," I yelled over to the shipping foreman where I work.

This exchange would take place just about every Monday morning as I passed his desk. Bob was a lot of things I'm not; tough as nails, missing a few teeth and occasionally acquainted with a bar room brew-ha-ha. His favorite players were ruffians like The Hound and The Hammer. He was definitely more concerned with who pounded who, than highlight reel goals- those were for sissies as he put it. Opening a can of whoop-ass was Bob's style of hockey.

While I could name the top 10 in scoring, Bob could name the top 10 penalty leaders. One year we tried to convince him to play in our golf league. His reply was perfect, "I'll start playing golf when I can physically stop my opponent from getting the ball in the hole." His kids gave him a tape of The NHL's Greatest Fight's one Christmas and even he admitted after about 30 min.'s he had to turn it off. It was the only chink I ever saw in his armor.

The obvious dichotomy in why we enjoyed different aspects of this macho game begs the question; what is a true hockey fan? Am I less of a fan because I preferred watching the Flying Frenchmen rather than a game laden with malfeasance? It's safe to say no one doubts the passion of us fans who pay $150 to wear a sweater with our favorite players name on it - $300 if you want the fight strap version. (By the way the only reason I didn't get a Ruutu jersey was I was afraid he'd be traded - I'm not a total wimp.)

The truth is we watch this game for varying degrees of many reasons. It's the speed, strength, danger, skill, sacrifice and ok, I'll admit it, occasional fisticuffs. In what other sport can you try to decapitate your opponent and the worst that will happen to you is a two minute time out, five minutes if you've really been a bad boy! Hell, at least I spanked my kids. Maybe Bettman should issue the ref's paddles.

This brings us to a discussion of the gentleman who often times brought us to our feet when he wore the Indian Head, that very bad man known as Wiz. Anyone recall when he tied the game up against the Blues two years ago on Easter Sunday with a slap shot from the slot, with 20 seconds remaining? (How do I remember that and not what my wife asked me to bring home from the store five minutes ago?) How about when he pounded Jordan Tootoo two years ago after the final horn sounded?

Yes, Wiz was a "formerly" well liked player in Chicago - oddly enough for his toughness and hard nosed play. That being said, his hit was an obvious attempt to seriously injure an opponent who was not expecting a cheap shot from his former teammate. Seabs was scheduled to stand up in Wiz's wedding this summer, although something tells me Brent won't be renting a tuxedo at this point. The vicious assault in no way could be construed as just a hard check. Do we really want hockey to devolve into Ultimate Fighting on skates? (Of course Bob would have used the word - evolve.)

I read on a blog site that this type of behavior is a result of the instigator rule - not being able to jump in and defend a teammate getting pulverized. I don't buy that, if you're that upset about a play, take the penalty and drop the gloves. I'm not sure about thieves, but for the most part there is honor among hockey players. I actually would have loved to see a Wiz – Seab's bout. Wiz is a major dude with the fists, quite adept at haymakers and roundhouse rights. Now that's hockey!!

Being a Chicago homie I was obviously very pleased with the suspension. Not necessarily to punish the Duck who had resorted to "fowl" play, but to send a message around the NHL that cheap shots to the head will not be tolerated. Is hockey any for the better with a Marc Savard or Campbell out? What really irked me was Wiz's statement that he didn't think he did anything wrong with his assassination attempt. Kind of like the sibling who whines "He started it."

I did note one positive outcome of Wiz's terrorist attack. (Where's Janet Napolitano when you need her?) I'm pretty adept at reading lips. When Seabs went to the bench, one of the trainers appeared to ask him his name. I could be mistaken, but I'm quite certain he said, "Duncan Keith!" Now, if we can only get him to play like him.

There were plenty of fans on the blog sites that echoed Wiz's sentiment. I have to think these fans believe the Chiefs from the movie Slapshot, are the epitome of a hockey team, sans the strip teasing, pusillanimous pacifist Ned Braden of course. Actually, I started to worry about Eager when he took his jersey off in the penalty box! On a side note, didn't Ivanans look like the true essence of a hockey player? Killer Carlson got nothing on that mug.

The debate will continue to rage on about the violence in hockey. For those of you who think the crackdown on cheap shots is going to ruin the game - what other sport would you turn to? Football is close I guess, accept for the continual stop in play. No, I don't think the league has to be too concerned about losing you, who Dan Hicks would describe as "O'Reilly at the bar" type fans. (O'Reilly was singing, O'Reilly was swinging, says I'm gonna smash your face. O'Reilly was smashing his face.) I ask this question with some reservation; who would you rather see play a Ty Domi or a Dennis Savard, a Brian Watson or a Bobby Hull?

To all you meatballs out there telling me to take up squash or girls hockey etc., take heart. I do contain remnants of my Irish grandma's blood. We used to watch the game at her house during the Original Six days. She'd sit there knitting away, paying little attention to the game until the fists started flying. I swear, I recall her dropping her needles while throwing imaginary rights and lefts, with her face contorted in anger screaming hit em, kill em! God help the person who took her pew in church!

By the way, for those of you who don't think God would be a hockey fan consider this passage from Exodus 21:24 - "eye for eye, tooth for tooth, hand for hand, burn for burn, word for word, bruise for bruise." Try to convince me He was not describing a hockey game. Just a warning to my friends who would say "Jesus said to turn the other cheek" - the Bible clearly states when he returns you would be well advised to have your name in The Lambs Book of Life.

One thing that was undeniable for Bob and I - we both loved this game. When he passed away, I thought about wearing my Blackhawk jersey to the wake. After reconsidering, I thought that it might be a little disrespectful. I should have went with my gut, for when I walked into the funeral parlor there were at least 10 Hawk jersey's on friends and family. Some of those friends had attended a Hawk matinee that day, no doubt hoping for a fight. Mr. "Hockey's becoming to Soft" was laid to rest in his jersey.

Rest assured Bobby, hockey will always be contested on the "macho" side of the ledger. Violence will always be interspersed with what I consider the better part of the game. Indeed, take heart, even a panty waist like me realizes that every once and awhile, someone needs to get pounded out there. Although momentarily stunned, can you imagine what a Hulk Hogan would have done to Wiz after he shook his head a couple of times? Has anyone checked to see if Hulk can skate?

Keep your heads up Wiz and Alex. And to those of you macho men out there who think I'm too soft for applauding Ovechkin's and Wiz's suspension, well I guess there is just no other way to put it; "I hope a giant crab eats your face!"

4/06/10

Rainy days and Sundays always get me ....

One advantage of being married is that, (unless you're Chuck Norris), you get exposed to many different points of view. Marrying my blushing bride has resulted in me doing many things that I wouldn't have otherwise. Far from being known as a Renaissance man, I have advanced from my Cro-Magnon days.

For example, think of the diversity in movies you watch if you're married. Many films that I would never have picked out, I ended up thoroughly enjoying. "The Traveling Pants of the Ya-Ya Sisterhood," "Driving Miss Daisy," and "Legally Blonde," to name a few. On the other hand, Nathalie wouldn't have seen such classics as "Napoleon Dynamite," "Snow Dogs," or "Dumb and Dumber."

 A few years ago, after taking the dogs for their evening sniff fest, I hoped to catch the last quarter of the Bull's game while lying in bed. You can imagine my horror when I entered the bedroom, to discover Nathalie had put a Carpenter special on. My first thought, over my dead body, quickly changed to an ill thought out question – "Are you watching this?"

As I headed to the basement, I stopped long enough to listen to one song. I was hooked, ending up being transfixed by the melancholic voice and tragically shortened life of Karen Carpenter. Now don't go thinking Lindbloom's gone light in the loafers; I cut my teeth on Hendrix, The Dead, Zeppelin, the Who, Allman Brothers, Beaustock and Hot Tuna. Yet, I had to admit, that documentary beat the hell out of a meaningless basketball game.

Her song, slightly re-titled "Rainy Days and Sundays Always Get Me Down," struck me as I watched the somber and morose crowd file out of The Madhouse last Sunday, into the post game precipitation. Was the Red Wing jinx still alive? You could just sense the Hawk faithful thinking, which goalie is going to eventually put his finger in the dike? (Maybe we could put Versteeg in the net!) Actually, I left the U.C. quite upbeat, encouraged by the Hawks play in the third. When we needed to, we were able to put our foot on the accelerator. If only we had been driving a Prius. In fact, rather than humming Karen Carpenter's lament, I found myself focusing on a song by Ian Dury and the Blockheads, "Reasons to be cheerful, part three."

Reason #1 – "I'm back and I'm jacked!" - The long awaited return of Burr-dog, inspirational speaker and hockey agitator extraordinaire. Adam has turned out to be that rare combination of speed, skill, brutality and lady slayer that is the mark of a NHL great. During the playoffs last year he was playing the best hockey of his career. His physical ability finally caught up to his loquaciousness. Generally not known as a player who quietly goes about his business, it will be interesting to see how he blends into this team.

If he still has that burst of speed he seemingly acquired out of nowhere at the end of last season, a Big Buff, Gentle Ben, Burr-dog line could contribute significantly to the teams post season success. This rabble rousing threesome is capable of fomenting considerable unrest in our opposition. The two players Burrish said he studied while rehabilitating were Toews, and this might shock you, Eager. Not a bad combination. Keep those skates and fists pumping!

Reason #2 – A good friend of mine, Tom O'C, has actually said two intelligent things in his life. First, "I'll never go backpacking with Wrong Way Delaney again." (That's a whole story in itself.) Secondly when I asked him about the Hawk goal tending situation, he brilliantly put it this way "We'd be in trouble if we had to rely on our goal tenders. The good thing is we don't." While on the subject of our beleaguered net minders, 56 year fan RoseLee noted of the second period, "The defense looked like they left the scene of a hit and run accident last Sunday."

Another thing I pointed out to some Doubting Thomas's is in the playoffs the forwards back check with considerably more "gusto" (Also known as the Schlitz back check.) How many times in the regular season do you see a player, other than Ladd, come back to help out like Kaner did on Crosby in the gold medal game. There's a reason most playoff games are not shootouts at the OK Corral.

What I find most irritating in our goal tending Soap Opera is when a semi-knowledgeable fan says, "Roenick said…" or "Pang said…" the Hawks don't have the goal tending to win the Cup. It's as if by mentioning a former players name their opinion increases exponentially in perspicacity. Granted, Roenick may have a little more room to criticize than most of us.

However, after listening to his color commentary during the Olympics, I couldn't help but think of drawing a Terry Bradshaw comparison. Like the "Hoot" who led the Steelers to a few Super Bowls, Jeremy seems to say anything that comes into his mind. He announces like he played – with reckless abandon. Don't get me wrong, I love listening to his commentary – there is no doubt he adds color! Yet, I fear that if things started going wrong for his team, he could easily digress into whining like Cub announcer Ron Santo is known to do.

Three last thoughts on how to get Huet rolling. First, give Cristobal some crystal meth right after warm-ups. Two, holler, "Hip, hip Huet!" after every save. Finally change his # back to 38. The #39 has been jinxing him all year. By the way, I know all you tenders in the stand are aware of this – Luongo has been pulled in 3 of his last 8 starts. His last game he let in 4. Bad things happen to even the best in the game. Help me out here, are we the only fans in the league who think our goal tending sucks?

 Reason #3 – The Hawks certainly weren't intimidated by the punks from Vancouver. Seabrook pounding the rope a dope in front of the Canucks bench was a thing of beauty. Can you imagine Keith Magnuson sitting on the bench, doing nothing, while a teammate was getting treated like the boy toy he is? Buffs near bout with the twerp otherwise known as Burrows, made me think of a famous Caravaggio painting in Rome.

It's titled, David and the Head of Goliath. It was my favorite piece of art in all of Rome. Literally, I could stare at it for an hour. When punky left winger dropped his gloves after he knew the refs would intercede, I couldn't help but think, "Oh, what a great time for a reverse David and Goliath moment." Am I alone, or could some of you other fine art connoisseurs imagine Buff holding Burrows head up to the 300 section? We can dream can't we?

Reason #4 – Jonathan Toews; period. Are we fans in Chi-town lucky to have this, as Sam Fels once noted, "Abnormal freak of ability and maturity." Actually, we were watching Dumb and Dumber, (again), last Sunday and I said, "Doesn't Toews look like Jim Carey?" While I could never imagine Jonathan selling a beheaded canary to a blind person – there is no doubt he would have bumped off the endangered Snow Owl if it meant a win. ("We whacked their bird, they whacked ours. These guys are good." – or something along that line.) My daughter Taylor is somewhat enamored by Toews, which often times can help me motivate her when she's playing in all day Volley Ball tournaments.

The last match of the day the girls can find themselves dragging, acting like their tired. Rather then give her one of my famous "When I was a kid speeches," that's when I pull out my #19 sign. A sign that proclaims, "I spit on your block!" My pep speech goes something like this;

"Do you think Toews would be acting tired right now? Hell no! He'd be lacing them up tighter, he'd be saying climb on my back, and he'd be telling the limp wristed spikers on the other side of the net – "Not in my kitchen!" He'd be telling his teammates, "If your tired get off the ice, it will give me more room to create." He wouldn't have told Herb Brooks, "My name is Eruzione, and gasp, gasp, I play for team USA." Toews would have said, "Coach, can we please do 5 more suicides!" After going through this spiel one tourney I asked Taylor, Are you jacked up now!?"

She just shook her head and was probably thinking her father is a lunatic. One of the dads in the stands once stated "She might not be jacked, but I am!" Most of her team also smiled as Taylor turned three shades of red.

At any rate, (and I realize I lost most of the blood thirsty hockey fans with the first mention of Karen Carpenter), try and recall two years ago when we were hoping to make the playoffs. Now our main concern is wondering whether our net minders are too weak to win the Cup!

Two last musings; first, if the Hawks start reading their press clippings, were done. A player like Cooke on the Penguins does not read them. Secondly, we have a game breaker this year, my Reason to be Cheerful #5 – Marion Hossa. What a tremendous acquisition, one I'd take over Luongo or any other of the goaltenders you're all clamoring for, any day. I must admit, before this year, I had no idea how good he is.

Finally, I know there will be more than a few ruffians with Probert jerseys on singing a Carpenter song in the shower after they read this. That's assuming of course they can read. One last thing, never ask Chuck Norris if he's ever listened to a Carpenter song. If you do, the last thing on this earth that you'll hear is the whooshing sound of a round house kick to the head.

4/14/10

The Peace Train

No one likes us, I don't know why.
We may not be perfect, but heaven knows we try.
And all around, even our old friends put us down.
Let's drop the big one and see what happens. – Randy Newman

The song *"Political Science,"* penned by that short people discriminator, is as poignant today as it was when it was penned 38 years ago. Transcending the acid test of time, it's still as relevant as it was during the anti war protesting days of the 70's. The signing of the "whatever" treaty in Prague yesterday by presidents Obama and Medvedev, having something to do with reducing the big ones in our respective arsenals, has me thinking...

First, I'm somewhat terrified at the prospect of Obama changing the national anthem to Cat Steven's "Peace Train." Somehow, our incredible baritone belting out, "I believe something good has begun," will not have quite as stirring an effect as, "the Bombs bursting in air." Secondly, is it possible we're finally getting it in this "mixed up, mumbled up, shook up world," as Ray Davies would put it? Perhaps the lamb can lie down with the lion. Was Patton's mistrust of the Russians misguided? Shall we drop our big stick and just walk softly while singing "Cumbaya, my Lord, Cumbaya." Or, should we "Drop the big one and see what happens."

In a few days, the hockey equivalent of all out war will commence. The problem with the aforementioned No Nukes Treaty is that it was signed with both participants, or at least one for sure, having the fingers of one hand crossed behind their back. It really isn't worth the paper it's written on. As hockey resembles life in so many ways, we can draw some parallels when it comes to wishful treaties.

When you're battling for you playoff life against a team full of thugs like Cam Janssen, you better have a couple of the Hansen brothers from the Chiefs on your bench. Perhaps if President Obama was a hockey fan he might understand the real ways of the world. Can you imagine him sitting down with Coach Q and saying, "I think you need to set an example for the rest of the league; I think you need to play more spin-o-rama type players in the playoffs."

While observing Wednesday's slugfest, I couldn't help but draw a comparison between Iran's Ahmadinejad and that ruffian on the Blues who wears #55. (Don't let my screams of "hit em, kill em, you stink ref," fool you.

The wheels on the bus are always turning while I observe the controlled mayhem on ice.) Unstable and nozzle are two words that fairly accurately describe both those Neanderthals. Janssen is the type of player you hate, unless he's playing for your team. However, even if Janssen played for the Hawks I still think I'd hate him.

Actually, Wednesday's tussle with the street thugs from St. Louis could only be described by three words; WTF. If nothing else, we got our moneys worth. From Janssen's first shift on the ice, until the final seconds when Toews tried to hatch the puck, the game was action packed. I was brought to my feet more than Nancy Pelosi at Obama's State of the Union address. (For awhile there, I thought I was observing a jack in the box.)

Sam Fels brother, Adam, wrote a thought provoking piece on the Hawks next big rivalry when the Red Wings are finally admitted to the Old Folks Home. While paying deference to the great Blues/Hawk donnybrooks in years gone by, he sagaciously speculated the Kings might be the next team we love to hate. (Would that be considered an oxymoron?)

The Kings could be our first round opponent, which would no doubt accelerate our antipathy for them in a hurry. While mentioning some of the better King's knuckleheads, he failed to mention Wayne Simmonds who is so dark he resembles Darth Vader on skates in the Kings home uniform. He's a Janssen with talent and would quickly become one of the players you'd like to launch a beer bottle at. As the saying goes though, if you like goons, he's a very good goon. Hey Wayne, you're in LA; try a little 30 sun block already.

While not totally disagreeing with Adam, next year when we split up season tickets, I'll be sure to secure a couple of Blues games. They always seem to be a "bang" for your buck. I'm sure the refs and linesmen are not clamoring for work at these games. Also, with the Blues jettisoning some of the dead weight on their team, Tzachuk and Kariya, it should leave them some salary cap room. Hawk fans probably shouldn't be too concerned about this because the Blues organization would probably sign some more goons – how about Jordin Too Too or Jared Boll? Can you imagine those two players joining Janssen on a line? The Armageddon line comes to mind.

Sam Fels is my guru when it comes to gaining insight into the deeper meaning of hockey; however I "slightly" disagree with his assessment of Buff's defensive abilities. His tomahawk chop at the end of the game showed me some fire that for the past two seasons we all wished Dustin had. It was Buff's Teddy Roosevelt's moment – skate softly but carry a big stick.

Besides, from my angle, he appeared to be going for the puck! I can't believe I'm advocating this, but I wish Byfuglien had a little more Janssen in him. A mean, dirty, 260# thumper is not something other teams look forward to going into the corner with. Can you imagine what a monster we could create if Burrish inhabited Buff's body? (Would that monster be called a Pronger?)

Besides it appears that he's no more a defensive liability than Campbell or Cam Barker's inadequate replacement, Johnsson. Don't get me wrong, the Campbell/Hjarlmarrson tandem has been sorely missed since Ovechkin's dastardly deed. However, moving Buff to the blue line has proven to be his "Free Willy" moment. He just seems to have more fun back there.

Despite missing an open net, that would have eliminated Buff's gaffe that led to the penalty shot, Steegs looked like Mighty Mouse on the pond against the Blues. He may be the classic example of a puck hog, but at least he's a grease lightning puck hog. While realizing his reluctance to relinquish the puck can lead to some bad transitions for the opposition, Kris is most alive when the puck appears to be super glued to his stick. He resembles Dale Earnhardt Sr. the way he recklessly flies about the ice, a yee-ha, ride-em cowboy, approach to the game. To hell with the knowledgeable hockey people, keep going one on five Kris. You can do it!

A friend of mine recently dropped me a note, admitting that he was a bandwagon jumper. He confessed that up until last year, his excitement for the Hawks or knowledge of the game was non-existent. I loved his statement though that hockey was "a new side of sports that he didn't know existed." Dan Fox went so far as to say, "May our mothers fear that we have all become hockey fans!"

I only bring this up to say to all of you diehards in the 300 level and the remnant in Sec. 101, take it easy on these new converts. My old boss used to say, "There are 18000 Hawk fans and they go to every game." Admit it; it's kind of nice to see the Hawks on page one in the sport section every now and then. Or talk to someone like my friend who has discovered a hidden gem. I realize they weren't checking to see who won last nights Sharks/Canucks game at 5:30am this morning, but it's a start. It won't be long before they realize that more than Toews and Kane play for the Hawks. And a word to the wise for you newcomers; if someone tells you to meet them at the Hawk statue, don't go to the Jordan statue!

One last thing I'd like to mention about Wednesday's Blues departure party. I was fortunate enough to get to sit in the companies seats with some customers. My personal season tickets are way up in boonies, lined up with the goal that the Hawks shoot at for two periods. Row 16 between the benches gives you quite a different perspective. While you don't see the action at the nets with as much clarity, you often are privy to some of the peace negotiations that take place as the players change shifts.

Colin Fraser's attempted negotiations with Cam Janssen were a classic example of why I don't trust the Russians. No matter how much Colin tried to reason with Janssen, he just didn't seem to get it. It's always close to a "drop the big one and see what happens" moment.

So, while Pres. Obama continues to try to reason with the goons of the earth, take heart Hawk fans. As long as there are Janssen's in the league, we'll be keeping our "nukes," those Ambassadors that negotiate in front of the benches – the Burrish's, Sopels, Frasers and Eagers. Hockey is war, let the battles begin.

In the semi immortal words of Martin Mull;

Might be those Red Chinese drop it first,
or those screw ball friends of Patty Hearst,
excuse me if I seem a touch blasé.
No, I never worry, bout getting bombed,
no, no I'm usually bombed anyway

Bombs away! Drop the puck and let's see what happens.

4/19/10

The Twelve Step Program.

"Hi, my names Rich and I'm a hockeyholic," I sheepishly admitted.

"Hi Rich," replied the other 12 balding, toothless, beer belly, Indian Head tattooed addicts in my support group. I joined this group last year after devoting way too much of my spring to late night games from the west coast. "Never again will I devote such time, energy and emotion to such a fruitless avocation," I thought. I learned way too much about unshaven Flames and Canucks, developing an unhealthy hatred for the numerous nozzles on those two teams. (You know you're in a bad way when you try to encourage our Hispanic fans to construct a Burrows piñata.)

As Ben Hogan once advised, I never did stop and smell the flowers last spring.

An avid reader, I digressed to anxiously awaiting the next issue of The Committed Indian. Another sign that you have a problem is when you tell your friends that Sam Fels's piece, entitled "Adam Burrish, Inspirational Speaker," was the best thing you read all year! The "Talk to the Ice Crew" tidbits should have won a literary award. When the 08/09 season finally ended on a fluke bounce off the backboard in Detroit, I realized I needed to seek help.

I discovered my addiction was fueled by hanging out with other hockey addicts whose main concern in life is to trounce the Red Wings and their condescending fans. When most of your waking hours are spent discussing the Hawk's goaltending issues, you're in a bad way – seek help. Huet's foot save in the final seconds of regulation of game 5 (?) against the loathed Wings is etched upon my mind. It's probably why I've defended him to the point of being tarred and feathered this year.

In a slight relapse, I joined a fantasy hockey league this fall, under the guise of pretending it was something my daughter and I could do together. (I kicked Taylor out of a co-management position when she tried to draft all Hawk players!) I should have called my sponsor, but I thought, "Surely, just one wouldn't hurt anything." As they say, "ah slight the angle and slippery the slope." It wasn't long before I found myself consulting the "dailyfaceoff. com" web site every day around noon. I now know way too much about third and fourth line left wingers on the Oilers or Islanders.

Last spring I came to the realization that I had merely substituted one addiction for another. Golf used to be an obsession with me, as I desperately tried to get my handicap below 10. When my enabling daughter convinced me to get season tickets last year, I knew I couldn't afford both hobbies. Actually, I was so far gone that I told Nathalie all I wanted were hockey tickets in place of my Christmas, Birthday and Fathers Day presents.

I'm afraid with the drastically increased playoff and next season's ticket prices, I'll be forced to spend my kid's inheritance. Actually, a tip I learned in golf on focus, could help the Hawks in their trembling quest for the Cup. I promise, I'll seek help when the Hawk season ends. I mean it this time. Calling my sponsor would be fruitless at this point; he doesn't answer calls during the playoffs.

Let me ask you something; when I mention the word "focus" to you, what do you think about? I heard it put in terms that any golfer could easily relate to. You see a high handicapper looks down the fairway and sees a green. Although with his grotesque swing, aim is the least of his problems, he tries to hit the ball in that general direction. A 10 handicapper looks at the same green and divides it into four quadrants. He aims at the one with the pin in it, although that by no means is a guarantee he'll hit it. C'mon, admit you 10's out there. You're stuck with a lot of 59 foot putts and we all know that's a crap shoot. A pro looks at that green and looks at a single blade of grass; enough said.

Focus, in my opinion is what it will take to advance by the Predators. They know there the underdogs in this series, which really unnerves me. A cornered rat always fights hardest and we're all aware the corners are where many hockey games are won. Nashville can easily lull one to sleep with their disciplined style of play. They seem to be masters of the counter punch. They have done more for insomnia than Sominex or Tolstoy's War and Peace.

If the person next to you starts snoring, punch him in the face to get him back on track. He'll thank you for it. For us to advance we'll need to be looking at blades of grass, especially #31 our Antimatter. So let's get acquainted with those "Nashville Cats" from Smashville.

Actually Dumont, Erat, Sullivan and Suter all played for my Fantasy club this year. All four can wreak considerable havoc in the O-zone. They have two young players that may be a thorn in our side for years to come in Hornqvist -RW and Franson –D. Hornqvist tied Sullivan for the team lead in points (51) and was +18. Franson was a +15 playing on the Pred's second defensive unit. Legawand has always been a pain in the butt against us.

Jason Arnot, the 6'5", 220# center and captain, was the 7th pick in the 1993 draft for the Oilers. He's a perennial 60-70point man on a team that doesn't allow its forwards to go into the O-zone when they get a lead. Jordin Too Too is a lethal weapon on skates. He still has a propensity to hit anything that's moving on the ice with mal intent. Weber and Suter are an outstanding defensive tandem. Both played significant roles for USA and Canada in the Olympics. They have tremendous goaltending in Pekka Rinne, (If Pekka picked a peck of pickled peppers...) and Ellis. If it's a low scoring affair, a lot of us will develop stomach disorders over the next 10 days.

By the way, the Hawk organization is close to releasing a new movie called, "In Search of Troy Brouwer," shot somewhere over the Fiji Islands. None of us have a good feeling about his absence; it's obviously something serious. Actually it could involve a combination of any of the following – women, dogs, trains or jail. I see all the earmarks of a country song emerging from this puzzling development. We're all hoping, "on a wing and a prayer," the situation gets resolved before Friday.

Good grief Cristobal. I certainly don't want to add fuel to the fire of the smoldering goal tender dilemma, however take note of Huet's stats against the Preds this year. Huet was 3-2 with a 1.41 GAA and .940 save%. That being said, if the Hawks can't trade Huet and his ponderous contract next year, I have a preposterous idea. Start Huet in Rockford next year. Not that I still don't have faith in the scapegoat for all our problems, but with Niemi playing so well and Crawford as an adequate back up, it would free a lot of salary cap.

With the recent increases in ticket prices, the Hawks should be able to afford this. At this point I'd much prefer to keep Sharp, Hjarlmarrson, Byfuglien, Verstud etc., than our Charlie Brown goaltender that everyone is always picking on. As far as the playoffs go, Huet is a nice ace in the hole should we need him. He is not as my friend Brian insists, "The worst goalie ever!"

Just a few brief observations from Sunday's loss to the aging Red Wings; if # 19, Deputy Richochet Rabbit's shot doesn't hit a post and cross bar late in the third, we'd be playing Colorado. Also, Sharp needs to bury that chance in the second period. Bear in mind we out shot them 16-3 in the second period and came out on the short end with Eaves tapping in an unfortunate rebound. How many times do you think were going to lose a period with that big of a shot disparity?

A fan was almost praying in our sky box that we didn't have to face Detroit in the first round. I say bring the Scum on, if they get by the Coyotes. 21

shots on goal – ooh, I'm scared. The Wings had Hossa and Samuelson last year, please don't tell me they're stronger without them. While it's almost impossible to stop him, Toews actually did a great job "limiting" that Commie – dog, Datsyuk. Stop #13 and Zetterberg and I don't see the Wings lighting the lamp a lot. Dawg, we've got Colin Fraser!

Funny thing about the Pred's, I don't really hate them, yet. Also, as long as it comes in limited dosages, I can tolerate Country Music. As the saying goes, "there are two things I like about Dolly Parton." The Nitty Gritty Dirt Band had a great album in the 70's called, Will the Circle Be Unbroken. It was a collaborative effort with some of the great old country stars like Doc Watson, Earl Scruggs, Junior Huskey, Maybelle Carter, Roy Acuff and Merle Travis. There's a great song sung by Doc Watson on the album called "The Tennessee Stud." A line in the song goes –"Those redskin boys couldn't get my blood, cause I was a riding that Tennessee Stud." Hopefully the folks in Nashville will be singing "The old gray mare, she ain't what she used to be..." when the Hawks get through with them.

Nitty. Gritty. Dirt. It sounds a bit like a playoff game, doesn't it? There's no doubt in my mind that, as Doc would put it, 'they's got some good horse's on the Preds." Ride em hard Hawks.

By the way, just in case – the Hockeyholic hotline is 1-800 HIT-SOMEBODY.

4/22/10

Keep passing the open windows

I don't know that I've ever seen a Jodi Foster movie I didn't like. The line from the quirky Hotel New Hampshire, "Keep passing the open windows," is one that has stuck with me 20 years later. If ever there was a game that would convince you to jump, Tuesday nights lopsided affair was it. It was clearly an outhouse type of effort – out hit, out hustled, out maneuvered, out muscled, out shot, out smarted and seemingly out gunned.

Like an outhouse, the only way to describe the game was, "It Stunk!" Also, I'm beginning to think the boisterous crowd in Smashville sees this match up as nothing more than a continuation of the struggles associated with the Mason-Dixon Line. We can only hope and pray that Charlie Daniels is wrong when he hollers, "Look out boys, cuz the South's gonna do it again."

There was a good old boy that I sold steel to in the Sovereign State of Mississippi that once told me, "Rich, we didn't lose the Civil War, we just ran out of bullets." This was right after he asked our waiter if there was a tree outside he could hang a couple of Yankees on, loud enough for everyone in the restaurant to hear. This was not the type of restaurant you'd want to park a car with an Obama sticker on it. Although the bar was not called, "The Do Drop In," there were a lot of patrons with sunburned necks and a chick with green teeth..

Now I realize most of the Predator fans go to hockey games because they think it resembles NASCAR on skates and are attracted to high speed collisions. Also, watching Bubba pound Bobby Joe is a hoot. However, defeating the favored Blackhawk's will only serve to inflame the red state/ blue state mentality. The Hawks are actually involved in a much larger struggle than they can possibly imagine. It is incredibly important to make sure the South knows who won that war once and for all. Game one was not a propitious one for the Yanks from Chi – town.

When my son was about 8 years old he told me, "Dad, this was the worst day of my entire life." While the Hawks game may have not compared to Greg's bad day, it was truly a "sitting on the dock of the bay" type moment. There was only silence in the car as my daughter and I drove home from a friend's house, after being tortured for two and a half hours while watching the most depressing Hawk game ever. (Water boarding got nothing on that game.) "Dad, do you think we'll win Thursday?" Taylor despondently asked.

Richard (boom boom) Lindbloom

The only answer I could come up with was, "I don't know" – which led to a fitful sleep punctuated by nightmares every hour or so. I do know one thing, if we keep playing in the polite manner the games have been contested in so far, "Looks like nothings gonna change." Where are our rectal agitators? (aka - pain in the butts.) I'm half expecting players on both sides to apologize to each other for hard hits. So, while I'm "wallowing up to my neck in it," let's see if we can find a glimmer of hope heading into the next, biggest game of the season.

First off, as Samuel Johnson once noted, "The gallows doth wonderfully concentrate the mind." We most certainly can expect a more doggedly determined effort from our troops – when you reach rock bottom there is only one way to go. The Preds have been dominating the play along the boards and dictating the style of play; that crap has to stop. I once read in a Sergeant Striker comic book that you can't be an effective soldier until you realize your dead already. If you know your about to die, why not go out in a blaze of glory. Maybe Coach Q should read Kipling's poem, The Charge of the Light Brigade, before Thursdays tussle. I expect nothing less from the men with the Indian on their chest.

Secondly, if you had an electron microscope, you could unearth a few bright spots. (I know I'm reaching here.) Niemi has played like a playoff goalie despite having to deal with way to many bonehead plays by our tightly wound troops. As the saying goes, we appear to be as tight as a bull's ass. Before the series began, I told friends the reason I fear the Pred's was the preponderance of two on one attacks generated by their stay at home defense. They are masters of the odd man rush.

Legawand's goal was classic Predator hockey. The Hawk defensemen need to rely on the buddy system if they plan to stop these sneak attacks. So far Antti has saved more than one Hawk blue liner. Duncan Keith, for one, continues to play like the Norris trophy finalist, and appears to be singing that Disco classic, "Let's get physical, physical. Let me knock you on your arse." It seems he has delivered more bone jarring checks in the last three games than he did all season.

Also, Colin Fraser continues to sacrifice his body like a suicide bomber in Baghdad. Kris Versteeg continues to take crap from no one and refuses to believe the trap can't be figured out. "I view it as my personal Rubik Cube," noted the double edged sword. The Pekka pickled peppers dam will eventually burst – hopefully Thursday night.

If Burr-dog gets released from the pound, all hell could break loose in the South. Burr-dog has the ability to make Gettysburg a foot note in the North

82

vs. South disagreements. Think about the suave and debonair Rhett Butler. Seab's, who has just rejoined Keith, keeps singing "Reunited and it feels so good…" as our number one d-tandem tries to hold the rednecks at bay. I believe we'll eventually realize that chasing Suter or Weber behind their net is a waste of time. The Pred's are exiting their zone way too easily.

Lastly, if we swallow the olive, think of how much money will save on Rounds Two, Three and Four. There's always a silver lining if you look hard enough.

Actually Nashville's top d-tandem, Suter and Weber, have been tremendous - do those two ever make a mistake? Combined with the jolly green giant in the net, they form hockey's version of the Bermuda Triangle. The puck tends to disappear from frantically searching forwards around Nashville's goal. It truly is a war of attrition scoring when these three are on the pond.

Yet, take faith Hawk fans, eventually Mt. Everest will be brought to its knees by the combined effect of ice, wind and time. Clearly though, scoring on the Pred's will more resemble a game of bombardment than high light reel goals. Can you say "stick your nose in it?" Brad Paisley wrote a song that pretty much summarizes how to score on the Preds – "time to get a little mud on the tires."

By the way, is it just me or has anyone else noticed the growing number of black players in the league? I'm afraid it won't be long until bad rap replaces bad organ music in the hockey Arena's. So far in the battle of the bro's, Joel Ward has a decisive advantage over Big Buff. The guy just never stops. While realizing he's a Canadian, with his work ethic I'd have to wager he'd most likely would have voted for George Bush. I know things are taking place at speeds I could not begin to fathom out there, but if Dustin had kept an eye on Ward instead of the puck, he might have been able to prevent Wards icebreaker in the first period. Forget that psychological babble; little things make a huge difference at this juncture of the season. Start sweating the small stuff, Buff. Somehow we need to get our big fellow fired up.

Hopefully, when the Hawks take the ice on Thursday they will have had a strong response to the question, "Do you have any last words?" Otherwise, it will be a long summer of Gin and Misery.

4/26/10

A Magical Moment – the disappearing puck trick.

Actually, the only way to describe Saturday's improbable victory is to let someone like boxing impresario Don King attempt to describe it. How about something along the lines of, "The ultimate, penultimate, opportunical, ressurectional, energetical, victorial game!"? Then again even he might not be able to invent words to describe it. Are hockey fans blessed with a rudimentary brain? How else can you explain most of us had not turned our TV's off in utter disgust when Hossa got sent away to do hard time.

While basking in the glow of the incomprehensible comeback Saturday evening, the memories of an old friend surfaced to the forefront of my meandering thoughts. Mike Szczepaniak, or Ears as he was affectionately called, is the epitome of a manic depressive Chicago sports fan. He has the innate ability to make Eeyore look like the life of the party. At 57years old, he's witnessed way too many collapses by various Chicago sport teams.

As a self defense mechanism, he has adopted the coping technique of saying the games over, (whether it be first quarter, first period or first inning), at the first sign of trouble. At times the weight of watching a game with him could become oppressive. The referee's or umpires were a constant target of his derision. I recall him, with squinting his eyes, questioning the calls of the umpire from the second balcony in old Comiskey Park. Until this day when I bring this memory up, Ears will say, "And the funny thing was, I was right!"

Without a doubt, when Legawand scored at the 6:23 mark of the first, Ears was saying well that's it, the seasons over. When Erath scored the lead goal at the 11:39 mark of the third, I'm pretty sure Ears was preparing to join Billy Joe McCallister in jumping off the Tallahatchie Bridge. Any of the four vituperative epitaphs would have been streaming from his mouth;

1. The Hawks don't care – if they can't get up for a game like this…

2. You can't beat luck.

3. The refs or the league wanted Nashville to win.

4. We should have played Huet. Quenville cost them the game.

I only bring this up because I thought about not only what this game must have done to his internal constitution, but the effect of the ebb and flow of this entire series with the Pest-a-tors. As Warren Zevon penned, "She put me through some changes Lord, sort of like a waring blender." It is on my too do list to check up on Ears to see if he or his TV survived this often times tortuous affair. Like Angela in the sitcom The Office, I to would have burned the book The DaVinci Code. Actually the scene in the book where the priest is whipping himself, reminded me of my tormented friend. For Ears, watching the various Chicago Sports teams comes about as close as you can get to self-flagellation.

Ah, but when things are going good! No doubt, Ears had a smile as wide as the Grand Canyon after Hossa hammered home the deflection of Sopel's shot, justification to Ears no doubt that the referee's got the call wrong. No one could have been more ecstatic than Marion after he found himself in the time out box, painfully pondering the evils of his way in the final minute of regulation. I'm sure Ears would have been calling the referee's every name in the book; "You don't make that call in a playoff game. It's not Hossa's fault that Hamhuis doesn't know how to skate – and besides Hamhuis had the puck. At worst it should have been a two minute penalty. If you have the puck, expect to get hit."

Actually, as I perused the Sports sections of the various newspapers Sunday, I was totally perplexed by the writers saying it's about time Hossa started earning his salary. Are those writers watching the same game I am? Hossa's skill, effort, defense and hustle have been good as anyone I've seen as a Hawk. It's a thrill to watch a multi millionaire get back on defense like the # 81 car. Does any sportswriter believe we'd be in the position we are without Hossa? Please!

John Madden was close as you can get to spectacular, and still be classified a grinder, while helping to stave off the 4 minutes of Pest-a-tor power play in the OT. There are so many little things that don't show up on a score sheet that contribute to a team's success. Mad-dog exemplifies the consummate team player, realizing what it takes to win at this level. If it weren't for a tremendous save by Rinne on Madden during the penalty kill, Hossa would not have had the chance to silence his critics (?). Hey, here's a wild idea – how about putting Madden-Kane and Steegs on a line together as a change up. I'm thinking, "The Limo Line" would strike fear in the hearts of fathers everywhere.

Kopecky's goal was one that resulted from that age old hockey adage, "keep your legs pumping." It didn't' appear anything would come of this play as he chased down the puck near the left dashboard. When he reached the puck he appeared to be sling shotted like a bat out of hell as he picked a Pekka's pocket. It appeared Rinne thought Suter was going to be able to cut him off. At the speeds that this incredible game is played at in the playoffs, if you go brain dead for a moment the puck very well could end up tickling the twine. Kopecks, who has been the object of considerable derision throughout the season, continues to gain supporters among the Doubting Tomas's out there in the 300 section world.

If Kopeck's goal was a beauty, Erath's first tally in the third was the beast that momentarily brought total darkness upon the land. What an incredible play as he caught the puck with his skate, kicked it to his stick and fired a wicked wrist shot past a bunch of dumbfounded Hawks. When he tallied the go ahead goal at the 11:39 mark all of us arm chair coaches were wondering how you could let a sniper like that get off uncontested shots from the slot. It appeared our coverage was discombobulated to say the least. As Bill Stortz would say, "We were as mixed up as Pedro's breakfast." Batten down the hatches boys.

A player who appears to be gaining supporters among the fault finders in the stands is the # 5 car. Forget about the blocked shots his aging body continues to absorb, I thought he was going to pull a spin-o-rama moments before Hossa's dagger. He skated around the Pred's net like a Brian Campbell impersonator, although he didn't look quite as smooth, taunting a confused Predator defense. You could almost sense the Pred's saying, "What the hell is that?" A friend of mine recently posed this question; "Doesn't Sopel look like he should be pulling a transmission out of a Mack truck, instead of being such a steadying influence on our back line?"

There is only one way to describe Niemi's stellar play in the net, the puck stops here! Antti has been awesome and it appears we have a Houdini in our midst. I'm sure it must have happened, yet I've never seen anything quite like the disappearing puck trick in my days of watching hockey. It was quite hysterical to see the homophobic Hawk players trying to locate the puck. I think Toews had his eyes closed as he delicately, at arm's length, reached into the front of Antti's bloomers. It added new meaning to the playoff adage, "You have to dig deep."

Well, our cardiac kids sure dug a little deeper in the final minute. The Fat Lady was not only singing, she was on the last verse! For the time being my friend Ears is stuck with a poop eating grin on his face. The only unfortunate part of the outcome was that I wasn't there. Oh, to bathe in the exuberance of such an improbable victory, to be in the joint when the players hoisted their tomahawks at center ice, to scream, to applaud, to hug a total stranger. It was as Brad Paisely sings, "there ain't nothing like finding twenty dollars in the pocket of the britches that you wore last week," type of moment.

It looks like Vancouver will be paying us a house call if we can put the final nail in the Pred's coffin. Funny thing about Nashville is that I still haven't developed a healthy hatred of them. In my mind, it's been a polite series. Even Hossa apologized for Hamhuis's lack of skating ability. I do know I'll have no problem garnering extreme disdain for the Canucks. I'm sure Ears, who won the MVP award in 1971 in the Catholic Hockey League while playing goalie for Mt. Carmel H.S., will be watching, cursing, laughing, crying, accusing and cheering those Red Men on.

Get the whips out!

5/3/10

The dark cloud of fear – "NUTS!"

In December, 1944, one of the greatest military battles in World War Two took place in the bucolic countryside of the Ardennes in Belgium. The Battle of the Bulge was called by many the turning point that hastened the inevitable surrender of the thinly stretched German forces. However, had Hitler's last ditch, desperate attempt to thwart the Allied advance succeeded, Belgium would most likely not be bilingual today – the incessant bickering between Wallonia and Flanders would have been resolved.

The ingenious plan devised by Hitler, against the wishes of his generals, was to launch a major counter offensive in the midst of one of the worst winters in the regions history. At his juncture of the war, surrender was not an option for Adolph. Hitler's aim was to split the British and American forces and cut off their only sensible point of supplies, the port of Antwerp. Without supplies, the Allied forces would not be able to advance into Germany.

Die Furher's plan was based on surprise, terrible weather and what he thought was the soft American GI. He also thought the Allied commanders could not launch a quick enough response to counteract the forceful thrust of the German might. The British and Americans were quite often at odds with each other as far as the recommended plan of attack. Fortunately for the Allied Forces, General Eisenhower didn't consult Congress before quickly assessing the dire situation.

John S. D. Eisenhower's book, *"The Bitter Woods,"* describes what transpired when the commanders of the Allied forces realized what was happening. Basically, they knew they were in big trouble. No one expected the German's to go on the offensive since they had been hightailing it back to the Fatherland as the Allies kept tightening the noose during their forward advance. When Eisenhower hastily assembled his commanders he could see that worry permeated the room.

His statement to the leaders could be good advice to our warriors in Game Two; "The present situation is to be regarded as one of opportunity for us and not of disaster. There will be only cheerful faces at this conference table." Within two days the Americans had moved 400,000 GI's into the arena to try to contain the German advance. A commander in the town of Bastogne was completely surrounded by hostile forces calling for his surrender. The commanders reply, "**NUTS!**" Hitler was about to find out a thing or two about what he considered the soft American soldier. I certainly expect nothing less from the Hawks.

Playoff hockey bears a resemblance to this historic conflict. Vancouver's initial thrust certainly has impeded our forward progress towards the Cup. While the Nuck's have taken the offensive in game one, there's still a lot of ground to cover before they reach Antwerp. An old grizzled veteran I used to work with named Chester, pointed out one of the strength's of the American GI, namely his ability to think for himself and adjust quickly to changing circumstances.

The Battle of the Bulge was won by pockets of soldiers, who although vastly out numbered and out gunned, managed to hold a town or crucial bridge until reinforcements could arrive. It wasn't without a heavy toll; there were over 77,000 casualties in this battle. A heavy toll is often what it takes to eventually hoist the Stanley Cup – dig in boys!

Chester, or the Gump as we called him, used to attend Hawk games back in the 1950's. He told me he and his brother used to heat up nickels and throw them out on the ice. I exclaimed, "Chester, you could have ended someone's career doing that." He just smiled, shrugged and said, "Ah, it didn't matter. They stunk back then."

While they may have not been heating up nickels, the sportswriters in the various Chicago papers were ridiculously negative after Saturday's, closer than the final score, affair. Most of them put it in the Grinch who stole Christmas's words; Stink, Stank, Stunk. Indeed if you looked only at the final score, the game resembled the situation where someone lets one fly in a car and quickly all four windows are lowered, despite subzero temperatures.

I missed the first period because I was barbecuing for my son's baseball game of the week. The aroma of dogs, brats, burgers and jerk chicken permeated the air. As Gus from the sitcom Psych would say about the jerk chicken, "You know that's right." While stealthily sipping on a couple of Stella's, I lost track of time. It was then I got a phone call from my panicked daughter.

"Dad, are we going to be ok?" Taylor mournfully asked. As I was quickly thrust back to reality, I realized things were not going well for our forces in Bastogne. Taylor, in a voice that was more depressing than Emily Dickinson's, "Because I could not stop for death, he kindly stopped for me" poem, said we were down 2-0. No hill for a climber I thought as I hurriedly packed up and headed to a friend's house for periods 2 and 3.

Don told me that although we were down 2-0, we actually pressed the attack pretty well in period one. I'll take 17 shots on goal any day. As I watched the second and we went down 5-0, I can honestly say I thought our effort was there. Sometimes the other guy just beats you. As we listened to the morons calling the game on Versus, I wanted to crawl through the TV and physically beat them. "The only thing the Hawks were good at was giving up odd man rushes," said one of the savants.

What did the imbecile expect the Hawks to do, sit back and play defense while down 3-0? The only ones seemingly downplaying the lopsided final were the Nucks. Vigneault put it best "We were able to finish and they couldn't finish. They had some Grade-A chances and our goaltender bailed us out." That's the game I saw. We made a couple of mistakes and paid dearly for them.

If our sportswriters were the generals in charge in Bastogne, the white flag would have been waving. I read all the "woe is us" articles in various publications and I couldn't find one positive thing said about the Hawks. One writer, who has apparently covered the Cubs to long, was extremely pessimistic. Seriously, 'the series could be over by Friday?!" Look I realize if you were in attendance for that game you left a bit downtrodden. However, can you honestly say we ever quit that night? The most positive thing I read was a note from RoseLee. She has seen more than one or two disappointments in her 50 plus years of riding the roller coaster known as Blackhawk hockey. "I think it said something that the seats remained pretty full until about the last two minutes... I thought it was sort of a comment on what they had given us all season...not to turn on them on this dismal night," noted long time season ticket holder.

News Flash: the war is not over. It has only begun. Patton is heading up from the South and Monty is closing in from the North. It's time to open up a can of whoop ass.

I know all of you Hawk fans are bleeding right now. You'll have to accept the fact that the road to the Cup will be filled with setbacks and disappointments. Save your pessimism for the Cubs or Sox. I think any knowledgeable fan knows that we're one of 8 very good hockey teams left. It's very wishful thinking to consider the Hawks are a favorite. Advancing to the Finals will be every bit as difficult as holding Bastogne. As Luongo noted, "It's just one game." While all may not be well on the Western Front at the moment, the battle has just begun.

Indeed as General Eisenhower might note "The present situation is to be regarded as one of opportunity..."

5/5/10

The Towel Trick!

Abraham Lincoln once noted, "It's better to keep your mouth shut and let people think you're a fool, than to speak up and leave no doubt." When I write about hockey I'm always treading on thin ice. When it comes to match ups, defensive positioning, saber metric's, floppers vs. butterflies etc., I don't have a clue. My hockey philosophy is basically skate hard and hit someone occasionally; oh yeah I almost forgot – Shoot!

As a friend recently put it, "I played the game with one philosophy...keep moving because a moving target is harder to hit." So, now that you've got my confession that I have no idea what I'm talking about, let me key in on a few moments that I felt were the turning point in Monday's game.

First, there was an early shift in period one that was a huge factor in a momentum change favoring the Hawks. It came after the Nucks hit the cross bar on a shot that would have given them a 3-0 lead. As the boys skated to the bench after suffocating the puck in the Nuck's zone for over half a minute, I hollered "Nice shift boys!" It seemed a lot of people in the sections around us echoed the same sentiment, as we gave our grinding warriors a mini standing ovation.

While nothing compares to the elation of finally denting the twine, it was obvious that the effort was greatly appreciated. Call it lunch pail hockey if you want to, the bottom line is we put our hard hats on and went to work. It was one of those moments that Chris Block mentioned is required to advance to the next round - "a willingness to take the game to the tough areas."

The outcomes of most games are determined in those little battles, the intangible areas that never show up in the stats. These moments tend to be the catalyst's that can often be the difference between a W or a L. One of the great things about being at the U.C. is that you notice more of the little things that go on during a game. The snarly attitudes (Bolland), the Free Bird (Steegs), the abominable snow shower (Burrish/Eager), an indomitable spirit (Ladd), the desire to get back on defense (Hossa, et. al.) or the willingness of a defenseman to absorb a pulverizing check behind our net. (Campbell/Hendry).

The much maligned Dave Bolland played Game Two like he had a bug up his proverbial butt. He was just plain ornery. I guarantee you; somebody pooped in his Cheerio's that morning. I had forgot he had a beautiful assist on the # 7 cars goal, and still thought he was one of the main dogs on the ice for us Monday. With the doggedly determined effort of his line mates, Versteeg and Ladd, they held the Swedish Sauna line to a total of 5 shots on goal!

There were many little things to enjoy at the game, but one of my favorites was when Mighty Mouse gave Samuelson one last facial as the refs tried to maintain order. I'm pretty sure dropping the gloves is not Bolland's forte, but he would have been a handful on Monday. A Hannibal Lechter move was not out of the question. On a night when all 4 of our lines were rolling, this line dug a little deeper. Andrew Ladd played like someone who wants to win another Stanley Cup. I'm sure it took a twelve pack and a long limo ride for Steegs to finally fall asleep after his game winning dagger.

A little thing I saw the Blackhawk's favorite whipping boy, Byfuglien, do happened behind our net in the second period. Rypien, who always skates as hard as anyone on the ice, was ticked off about something Dustin did. He unwisely tried to hit Buff head on behind our net, to try to even whatever score it was he was trying to settle. It was perhaps the biggest collision of the night. Rypien might be well advised to bring a yacht to Chi-town next time he wants to go sailing. Buff also seemed to fit into the Toews – Kane equation. Keeping my fingers crossed on the potential of that threesome on Wednesday. Oh Buff's got a big old butt, oh yeah!

When Adam Burrish went down in preseason with the knee injury I thought to myself, "What the heck am I going to write about this year?" He's just one of those characters who seem to give you never ending copy. He's a walking advertisement for Viagra. Monday's game was Classic Burr Dog.

While Vancouver may have the gay Green Men, (those two are not right) we have Dumb and Dumber on our bench. It's hard to measure the impact their one sided conversation with Burrows had on the game, but I guarantee you it contributed. At the very least it turned a tense crowd and team into one that was smiling. I don't care what you do, if you're smiling your half way there. Eager was trying to chime in but it appeared he was laughing too hard at whatever it was Adam was discussing with Alexandre. I'm pretty sure they were not discussing Einstein's Theory of Relativity, although the conversation may have included some of Alex's relatives.

Adam's second huge contribution was when he gave Luongo a snow shower. Actually I thought he did it in tandem with Eag's which made it twice as funny. A double your pleasure, double your fun type moment! To me, it was the turning point in the game. It evoked a surprisingly tepid response from the Canucks. Granted, Luongo eked a measure of revenge when he stopped the # 37 car's break away. If Adam had just thrown the puck a little more toward the post instead of the middle of the net, the United Center would have self-imploded.

As Sam Fels once penned – "You can't stop Burr-wood." Actually, and this is pretty scary, there seemed to be a chemistry on the Dumb, Dumber, Dumbest Line. One thing that is indisputable is that Madden and Burrish love playing this game. By the way Eag's, when you raise your hand get off the ice dawg!

Was it just me or did the referee, # 11 Kelly Sutherland, seem to take great delight in calling penalties on the Hawks? He was an irritation most of the night, which reminds me of a comment RoseLee's son, Larry, made awhile back that still has me chuckling. When we discussed whether or not Lysiak actually tripped linesman Ron Foyt, Larry said, "Lysiak was justified in tripping him, he was terrible all night." Back in the days when they only had one ref trying to keep law and order on the ice, my brother John would moan when the referee's took the ice, "Oh no not that bum Ashley." If you can actually discuss the referee's abilities or know them by name, seek help!

Someone is going to have to help me out here and tell me why Sharp was not the number one star. I know I'm given to hyperbole, but that may have been the best game Sharp has ever played for us. His name almost changed to "Rufio" when he narrowly missed going top shelf on that second short handed effort. Hossa has been getting a lot of criticism for his lack of production in the playoffs. You may criticize his stats – but there is not a harder working player on the ice. Little things contribute enormously to the big picture. It's only a matter of time before he starts lighting the lamp.

While Luongo is not getting a sunburn from the lamp behind him, we seemed to turn up the heat significantly in Game Two. There's a song by Bruce Cockburn that describes the struggles of trying to score on Roberto - "Nothing worth having comes without some kind of fight, got to kick at the darkness till it bleeds daylight." All of our goals were from within 15 feet – I think I'm seeing a pattern develop here.

Niemi was outstanding, although I know I wasn't the only one holding my breath on Monday. He made two smoking glove saves from less than 20 feet to keep us in the game before Limo man pierced the souls of the Vancouver faithful. There's a good chance they were passed out by this point anyway.

As we drove home I told a friend, you know the Canuck fans started drinking like fish when they went up 2-0. "No doubt the Yukon Jack was being passed around," said Jim. There's just something about this game that evokes emotion like no other. When we score, especially a crucial goal, we don't cheer; we explode and then head to the refrigerator. How else can you explain people parting with the treasured rally towels, momentarily turning the ice scarlet? On Towel Trick Night, it seemed to finally be bleeding a little daylight.

"Nice shift boys!"

5/4/10

Peace negotiations

Possible things Burr-dog and Ben Eager were saying to Alexandre Burrows. You have to look at the picture on page 96 of the Hawkeytown magazine. Scott Strazzante's photo may be the greatest hockey picture of all time.

"Hey Alex – you want one lump or two – and I'm not talking about in your tea, twerp."
"Hey Alex – all roads lead to Burr-dog."
"Hey ho-bag – look at me when I'm talking to you."
"Hey Alex – there's a great bar in the Chi for you – The Open Closet."
"Hey Alex – how's about Dr. Burr-wood perform a little plastic surgery on that ugly mug."
"Hey Alex – "this is Eag's – your mama."
"Hey Alex – "Eag's again – your sister."
"Shut up Eags, that's my ho."
"Hey Alex – Its hair appointment time." Eags, put your skate back on, no Happy Gilmoring on him.
"Hey Alex – what we have hear is a failure to communicate" – (Cool Hand Adam)
"Clarice"
Hey Alex –do you like banjo music – da da da, da, da. I play the banjo and you squeal like the pig."
"Hey Alex – "we got no food, we got no jobs, are pets heads are falling off – but were still your worst nightmare."
Hey Alex – give us your lunch money. We'll put it towards your elevator pass.

5/7/10

The # 13 and Ivory Soap – a contrast in taste

Forget about the numerous Elvis sightings, did anyone else besides me notice that an Orca impersonator sang Canada's national anthem? While the tuxedo festooned singer did a better job than the guy who tried to speed sing our national anthem, the best part of either of the songs was when the crowd belted it out. I never realized just how good we have it with the booming baritone, Jim Cornelison. Makes me wonder how many rinks you could visit and hear such a heart rendering rendition, one that gives you goose bumps – and I'm just talking about when he sings "Oh Canada." The "bombs bursting in air" are not the only thing booming when Cornelison grabs the microphone.

Well, where do we start when beginning to describe Wednesday's gala affair? Probably the best way is too jump ahead to Thursday morning. Somewhat of a health nut, I found myself at McDonald's drive-through ordering perhaps the unhealthiest meal one can ingest – the #13. (Why is it when something tastes good, it's probably bad for you?) Obviously, I had one to many while watching the game at a friend's who didn't know when to cut me off. That's right Don, it's your fault. While we didn't resort to shots of Yukon Jack, we did put a serious dent in Don's Stella Artois supply. I'll never do that again and this time I mean it.

The picture of the year appeared in Wednesday's morning Trib. (Located on page 96 of the Hawkeytown magazine.) For all you nerds out there, and I think you know who you are, tell me the two characters chatting with Burrows did not take your lunch money, or make you buy an elevator pass in high school. I've never been a big fan of bullies, but someone needs to send a stern message to Burrows besides Dave Bolland. As Dumb and Dumber might put it, "Put another Nuck on the Barbie!"

I've finally found someone to loathe more than Cam Janssen on the Blues. When Burrows skated over to save Daniel.Sedin from Dave "the Undertaker" Bolland, trying to repeatedly slam the # 36 cars head into the dash board, I began to wonder if I was watching tag team wrestling. I fully expected him to skate over to the Canuck bench and pull out a ladder to ram Boll's with or bang him over the head with a chair.

Alexandre Burrows clearly has a future in the WWF if the hockey thing doesn't work out. Also, will someone please tell me why Bolland got a penalty because Sedin put his stick between his legs just prior to the face off? I'm thinking that's not a desirable position. I'm hoping the NHL doesn't consider suspending the Hawks new enforcer. "In this corner..." Keep snarling Dave!

I'm not sure if it was all those white flags, err I mean towels waving in the air, but it truly is a travesty to see a Canadian lose his "cool." The Canucks appeared only to be a slightly more talented version of the St. Louis Blues by the time the final horn sounded. I realize it's important not to get overconfident in this series, we all know Lady Momentum is a fickle mistress. It was only one game and you can be sure the Nucks will be packing on Friday. I'm not sure about the Sedin's, but you know Alexandre will have some brass knuckles or razor blades tucked somewhere in a body cavity. The key to Friday's game was given to me by Larry Deutsch, "Kiss. Keep it simple Steeger. When we do we're really smart. When we don't, the puck ends up in our net or zone for a long time."

Anyone who knows me will tell you I'm no braniac. However, I'm thinking it's not a real good strategy to get By-foog-lee-un all riled up. Let a sleeping dawg lie. (Wonder if Vigneault is regretting mockingly pronouncing Dustin's name?) Larry's funniest comment was about our suddenly aroused sleeping giant, The Buffster. "Buff got jobbed with his penalty after the raking he took to his face, but did you see how he held one Canuck with his right arm while punching another with his left. I laughed out loud. I think he was going for the Gordie Howe hat trick - a goal, an assist and a fight.

Another thing Larry pointed out was none of the goals resulted from slap shots. (I guess you might argue Buff's first did after Luongo couldn't control Keith's blast.) They mostly resulted from wandering into the tough areas and from hard work along the boards. Ladd's work on Steegers "blast" and Toews board work on Buff's third goal were great examples of rolling your shirt sleeves up. As Eddie O pointed out, Ladd is skating in straight lines!

While on the subject of straight lines, the battle between the pipes surprisingly tilted in favor of the Hawks on Wednesday. I realize Roberto is one of the best, but it appears from this mild mannered reporter's observations, there are some chinks in the armor. The Jester has Lost His Jingle, so to speak. I thought Charles Barkely was known as "The Round Mound of Rebound." I'm not sure that Antti has another first period like last game, but if it's half as good we'd be ok. When's the last time you saw a Hawk goaltender take over a playoff game? I'm thinking – Tony-O. Anti not only repelled the kitchen sink, he turned away the Butcher, the Baker and the Candlestick Maker. Then he jumped over the moon!

The special team's battle has been interesting. If you're Vancouver, you might want to decline the penalty when Hossa/Toews or Sharp/Versteeg are penalty killing. Toews and Hossa have been eerie on the kill. As

Bazooka Joe would note, while everyone else was in sitting, Sopel and Hjarlmarrson have been outstanding. Our power play has been surprisingly effective, although Vigneault has been claiming it closer resembles a bulldozer play. I'm not sure what he meant when he said Toews pitch forked Luongo, but I don't think it was a compliment.

Tonight's contest has all the makings of a donnybrook developing. I'm sure Jimmy "the Mouth of the South" Hart (Burrows) will be on his worst behavior. It will be interesting to see if D. Sedin decides to continue his dastardly ways. Let me think, if I had to choose between "Daniel the Scorer" or "Daniel the Enforcer" it's a no brainer.

While on the subject of no brainers, if the referee's let this get out of hand, it could turn ugly. I'm thinking that maybe the refs should have a bar of soap handy in case the language deteriorates. The potential of a very physical contest tonight reminds me of a friend I brought to the game on Monday night. He's not what I would call a fanatical, statistical, eat, sleep and drink hockey fan; but boy did he chuckle when some poor unfortunate soul out there got blasted! Dump it deep and hit someone. Skate in straight lines. Call your mom!

To all you mom's out there who improved our command of the English language with Ivory soap – a very Happy Mother's Day. (Even Mrs. Burrows.)

5/11/10

"Everybody's Dreaming Big" - Sugarland

Have you ever had a really weird dream? One of those where you try to solve a problem - but are continually confounded? Well, welcome to my daughter Taylor's world. After Friday night's game she told me she dreamt she was on a line with Toews and Kane. Apparently they were not pleased with her effort, often times rolling their impatient eyes in disgust.

At one point they were yelling at her to ice the puck. It was then that she explained to them she had a rubber stick – and every time she'd try to shoot the puck the stick would bend. Kaner went to the bench and then threw her a stick saying, "there use that one." As Taylor's nightmare progressed she hollered over to them, "It's a right handed stick, I'm a left wing. Duh!"

Until Taylor gets her equipment situation straightened out, I don't think Buff has to worry about being demoted to another line. He's been a notoriously Big factor in this series. The restraint he showed when O'Brien cross checked him twice and then raked his helmet off was nothing short of remarkable. If he had got up and fought the misbehaving Canuck, both would have probably been sent to the time out corner for roughing.

Instead, the penalty led to an early momentum changing power play goal. It's probably a good thing O'Brien kept assaulting Buff, it appeared the referee missed the first two cross checks. Watching Buffy get under the Nuck's skin has been a thing of beauty. I'm thinking if Dustin dyed his hair blonde or pink, he could give Dennis Rodman a run for his money in Chicago sports lore.

"Playing guitar like a ringing a bell," Jonny has been better than good. My boss asked me a question after game 2, "Who do you think is better, Toews or Kane?" Have any of you Blackhawk fans come up with the answer to that one yet? At first glance, one quickly notes Toews's all around play – scoring, face offs, maturity, bulging muscles, psychotic intensity and defense – truly the total package.

Then you stop for a moment and think of all Kane's big goals, the magic he possesses when carrying the puck on the power play or his uncanny ability to make the front cover of the National Enquirer. Kane also has a very annoying knack, (for our foes), of stripping lumbering defensemen of the puck when it seems they've got to it first.

I suspect if a poll were taken to determine who would you rather have between those two, it might end up an even draw. The truth is, when they play together there is a synergistic effect similar to the Harlem Globetrotters Curly Neal and Meadowlark Lemon. That team is still undefeated!

Actually Toews was quoted after game 4 saying, "I've been trying not to just factor in how many goals I'm scoring to rate how I'm playing." One of those little factors in game 4 transpired in the last minute or so. Jordan Hendry, who had very limited ice time that game, added some fresh legs to our defense. There was one play behind our net where he skated at full speed, knowing he was entering the "I'm about to become a pancake zone."

The "impact" of that play will never show up in the stats, but the puck quickly exited our zone as a result. Actually, in Sunday night's loss, if I have one criticism it would be we avoided those life threatening moments. If we come out with more of an "I regret that I have but one life to give to the Hawks" attitude, we'll be okie dokie.

The difference in Game 4 in my book was the incredibly stupid penalties the Nuckleheads took. Help me out here, but was Vancouver trying to win a game or engage in a five on one beat down of Byfuglien? I'm not sure I've ever seen anything like it - there was not even an attempt to be discreet about it.

Thuggery, malfeasance, brutality and wickedness, are just some of the adjectives that describe the puzzling Vancouver game plan. They made Wisniewski's run at Seabrook look like a clean check! I don't mean to preach, but Burrows and O'Brien really need to peruse 1 Corinthians 13, the great "love is" chapter - "Love is patient, love is kind, love is long suffering..." The Canucks don't need a pep talk; they need a Bible study after game 4.

Luongo must have felt like the players in front of him were abandoning ship on Friday. Not sure I can blame Roberto, other than maybe Seabs twisted wrister, for the stinging defeat. In mythology, the story of Pandora's Box tries to explain how the world got so messed up. When the dimwitted Epimetheus (literally translated "thinks after."), opened the box, all the evils of the world were released - war, plagues, famine, disease and numerous other pestilences - most notably Burrows and O'Brien.

It sure helps explain the mess the Nucks found themselves in. The one good thing that emerged from the box was hope. You can bet your bottom dollar the Vancouver players were clinging to it as they headed into a must win situation on Sunday. We all know this is a very good team we're up against. While a little thinner on the blue line, their forwards are every bit as dangerous as our young guns. You don't want to let The Flash, Mason Raymond, get a full head of steam going – that Nuck accelerates like a Ferrari.

We needed something to get us going in Game 5. As the third period was about to commence, I asked Sam Fels to tell us a joke to loosen us up a bit. Section 320 appeared to be a little down in the dumps after the second period ended. We desperately needed someone to bring some light to the foreboding darkness around us. It was his Patrick Henry moment; unfortunately, he failed miserably! How about a little humming bird joke next time; "What did the Hummingbird have for lunch?" Give up? "A Hummmmmmmmmmburger."

After observing last night's game, it was somewhat hilarious listening to the "one shot of wine, two shots of gin," element giving their alcohol impaired viewpoints on the post game show. We weren't hitting (that's original), we were standing around to much and were slow (last call), we took stupid penalties (no, if you want to see what stupid penalties are, watch O'Brien or Burrows), we weren't ready (I think you might have hit the nail on the head – now whack yourself in the face with the hammer!), or we weren't creating a traffic jam in Luongo's kitchen (you are the reason traffic camera's have been installed at busy intersections.) As Bruce Cockburn sang – "If I had a rocket launcher, some son of a bitch would die."

From my perspective, it wasn't all that bad of a game. We had ample dangerous opportunities that Luongo thwarted, in a very solid performance. There were rebounds; they just didn't bounce our way last night. Our face offs were dismal in the 3rd during crunch time, Toews especially looking like a fool with his pants on the ground. (At least his helmet wasn't turned sideways and there was no detectable bling.) Our passing was not all that bad with the exception of when we entered the Nuck zone. We broke out of our zone pretty well all night. The biggest difference to me was pointed out in a song sung by old blue eyes that RoseLee mentioned;

"they call you lady luck, but there is room for doubt – at times you have a very un-lady-like way of running out."

There's just no other way to put this, last night Lady Luck was a tramp! Perhaps the Hawks could dwell on another movie classic on their four hour flight to Vancouver. It could very well shed light on their ticket to the Conference Finals. In the movie SPINAL TAP, an interviewer asked one of burnt to a crisp band member's, "What's the secret of your success?" Without hesitating he mumbled that there amplifiers go to volume 11, instead of 10.

Like I said, and I'm sure a lot of you disagree with me; I thought we played at level 10 last night. Not a bad volume, but we need to crank it up a notch. Let's play with a Killer Whale instinct in Game 6. I'm not to sure my internal constitution could handle a game seven.

We're all still dreaming big despite last night's setback. Big Dreams require Big Efforts and a willingness to enter the pancake zone. As my grandma would say, roll up those shirt sleeves and put a little elbow grease into it. The harder you work, the luckier you get.

Indeed, "Luck, be a lady tonight!"

5/10/10

Tough nuts to crack

The PGA shows a commercial that illustrates just how good professional golfers are. You get the feeling after watching the highlights that they're throwing darts, not playing golf. The commercial ends with the exclamation, "These guys are good!" After observing Sami Salo add intense new insight to the phrase, "fighting through the pain," perhaps the NHL should come up with a new slogan – "These guys are tough!"

When Duncan Keith's (who you gonna call, ball busters.) bunker buster brought Salo to his knees, there were two chances he would be dressing for Tuesdays game in Vancouver, slim and none. Playing over 19 minutes in that condition, deserves the Canadian Medal of Honor or knighthood or whatever it is they do in British Columbia.

Salo, could have easily taken a pass on game six. No one would have questioned his manhood, or sudden lack thereof. He came off for a shift in the first period and was wincing in obvious pain. Even Adam Burrish called the area a "no fly zone." If Sami were to sing Chuck Berry's classic "My Ding a Ling," he'd be hitting all the high notes! There's only one way to describe Salo's effort – "Now that's Hockey."

Finishing off the Nucks was a laborious process. The series reminded me of the movie, The Pit and the Pendulum, the way the momentum swung back and forth. (C'mon now, suck that stomach in.) It was emotionally draining for fans on both sides of the continental divide. Fans tend to get a little antsy in these series. Hawk announcers still bemoan the struggles we had dispatching the Preds, as if we were a heavy favorite. The desire to have their name inscribed on the Cup seems to supersede a paycheck for these warriors on skates – it greatly levels the playing field. Throw in a hot net minder and all our finger nails get a little shorter. (Caps and Peng's anyone!)

I'm reminded of Pope Julius yelling up to Michelangelo to hurry it up and finish when he was painting the Sistine Chapel. Can you imagine what the ceiling in that chapel might look like today in our age of instant gratification? Reaching the Stanley Cup Finals is every bit as tedious and painstaking as the four years it took to complete the Michelangelo's masterpiece. When players like Brouw, Eags, Kopecks, Hossa, Buff and Ladd finish their checks or head to the corners, it seems we gain a little more ground, another stroke of the brush in the big picture.

After the clincher on Tuesday, my heart went out to the Nuck's fans. Twenty minutes after the game, there were still scattered fans ensconced in their seats, seemingly too stunned to move. I noticed one girl who appeared to be trying to cheer up her disconsolate boy friend. She appeared to be saying, "It's ok honey, it will be all right; eventually." I thought Blackhawk fans were critics until I read the Nucksmisconduct web site. The backstabbers came out in force moments after the contest. I thought we were the only NHL fans that blamed the goaltender no matter what the circumstance.

News Flash: if you let snipers in the NHL fire at you from the slot at 10 paces, well you just might find out as Joe Jackson sang – "Jack, you dead."

I think the series boiled down to a seriously depleted defense core for the Nucks. Some of their third liners were forced to play big minutes against a Hawk offense that was firing on all 8 on Tuesday. Didn't Bieska just return from a serious injury weeks before the playoffs. I noticed he was logging over 25 min/game. Actually, the area along the boards and behind the net appeared to be where the Hawks finally prevailed. It seems like when we started dumping and crashing, we wreaked a lot of havoc in the Nuck zone.

Even so, the game wasn't as lopsided as the final score. The short handed dagger by Dave "the Undertaker" Boland was the play that really buried the green and blue men. Still, when O'Brien made it 3-1 on a great rush, we all took a big swig of our beers to calm the nerves. Ten shots in 7 minutes to open the third by Vancouver had us reaching for the valium bottles in The Big Chi.

Raymond was scary last night – I know this isn't a subject Nuck fans want to think about right now, but it's going to take a lot of money to sign The Flash. As much as I've come to loathe Burrows, he had a hell of a series when he wasn't trying to be a tag team wrestler. By the way, while I don't suspect the Canucks will be "parking cars and pumping gas," supposedly during the handshake Buff did ask Roberto, "Do you know the way to San Jose, I've been away so long ..."

Our much maligned third line continues to percolate. Versteeg had happy feet all night long. I recall writing two years ago that "you might be a Blackhawk fan if..." you realized Bolland and Versteeg were a notch below Toews and Kane. Granted, it's a big notch. As we are well aware, Steegs is only a notch above Eag's in the evolutionary scheme of things, but his heat seeking missile on the Hawks second tally was devastating.

Generally speaking getting the puck by Roberto requires all the finesse of a Rugby scrum. I loved the way Kaner celebrated after his sick wrister. At first when he pumped his fist by the glass, I thought he was trying to pull a Byfuglien and rile the crowd up. Upon further review, I saw a fan with that beautiful deep red jersey on that Patrick was pumping his fist at. The cost of that seat – priceless!

The only possible way to describe the metamorphosis that is known as Dustin Byfuglien is from the movie, MASTER OF DISGUISE. Pistacchio changes into a turban and repeats the mantra, "Become another person, become another person," and is transformed from a bumbling idiot into the Dali Lama. The only possible explanation that explains Buff's transformation from a distant, phlegmatic, laissez faire forward into what Jerry Lee Lewis would describe as a "goodness, gracious, great balls of fire" (sorry Salo) goal scorer is reincarnation.

Mean streak-check, crushing body collisions-check, big screen in the crease-check, borderline malfeasance-check, finally showing some emotion-check, a Lennie from Steinbeck's OF MICE AND MEN gone wild-check. I'm just praying they don't make him give a urine sample. As the song goes, "Back that butt up." Shake shake shake, shake your booty!

Two players who came up big on Tuesday were Sopel and Hendry. (Sounds like a law firm, doesn't it?) Chris Block noted that Vigneault would use his last call on the lines to try and match up the Sedin's with our third line defensive tandem, trying as best he could to keep The Swedish Sauna line from butting heads with Keith and Seabrook. It worked well in the first period and appeared to be an accident waiting to happen. Somehow we dodged that silver bullet. It should be noted, for the record, that both Sopel and Hendry worked their tails off. Although I did have to close my eyes at moments!

Niemi's eyes appear to be wide open. The "all in all it's just another puck in the wall" version of the Pink Floyd classic, seems to be an ever growing assessment of our net minder extraordinaire. Another way to put it is in the words of Rick James, "He's a brick, house!" (You know that's right.) As we jump out of the frying pan and into the Tank, I'm thinking a Fin is a good thing to have while navigating the shark infested waters. While admittedly a season long Huet supporter, its obvious Coach Q made the right choice finally deciding on the untested puck eater. (Think Pac Man) I saw him resort to his trademark "luge" save in game 6. It's when he scissors the his legs together, lifts his head and then watches the grinders on the opposition try to amputate his legs. Antti, it's time to FINnish the job you started.

My biggest concern going into Game One is a mental letdown after outlasting the Nucks. Will there be a sense of urgency or an attitude of "let's tread water" for awhile. It would be great to win the first game in one of these series. Will we ease up; back off so to speak from the intensity we had to summon in game 6? The last time I told someone to ease up was when we were sockeye salmon fishing in the beautiful Johnston Strait in British Columbia.

As my son Greg reeled a whopper up to the boat, the guide reached for the net. That's when I passed along the sagacious advice to Greg to ease up a little. I can still see the face of the guide, a face that screamed "Are you an idiot or what?" Needless to say, that sockeye got a free lunch that day.

There is no such thing as a free lunch during the playoffs. You only get so many chances to advance past the Conference Finals. This could be the first Original Six final since 1978 -79. Let's not fall back on the Cub's famous motto, "Wait until next year." The Hawks have a great chance to pull the fish into the boat now, if they don't ease up. From my days of watching Flipper, it should be noted that if a dolphin is swimming fast enough, he can kick a sharks butt. It's definitely not a good time to be treading water. For all you fans hoping for a quick series, get ready to suck that stomach in.

By the way, what did the shark say when he swam head on into the concrete wall – Dam!

5/17/10

The Color Teal

"Dude, your boy friends wearing teal!" - Sam Fels penned that line in one of his top ten things not to like about the Sharks last season. It's one of those lines that emit a muffled chuckle in our politically correct world. The color teal was a huge fashion success a few years back, but somehow I don't think you'd find it in Randy "Macho Man" Savage's closet. It reminded me of a moment not to long ago when I was picking out the colors for my daughters softball uniform.

As I recall, the 3 options on colors when it came to my choice were dark green, yellow or teal. Teal would have been my last choice but on a whim I asked one of the ladies coaching what she thought the girls would like before going with my gut, dark green. Both ladies I talked to without hesitation said, "Teal!", as if I was some sort of Neanderthal.

My wife and daughter echoed the ladies choice when I got home, quite astonished that I even had to ask for advice. Which leads me to the conclusion; a macho man did not design the Sharks uniform. No doubt Sean and Gus from the sitcom Psych would have no problem deducing that the Shark sweater was designed by a very gay man in San Francisco. They can slap as many sharks as they want on the sweater, it still reeks of pusillanimity. At least make the Shark look mean! Truly, Mack the Knife has left the building.

Scarlet billows began to spread early in Sunday's affair. "Gentle" Ben Eager tried to knock everything he saw in teal into the middle of next week. Had he played more than 6 minutes someone would have ended up in the hospital. Rumor has it after the game the Bay City Rollers were asking him if he knew how to roller skate. When questioned afterwards, Bennie told George the equipment manager, "I just want to pet the soft bunnies."

Actually, the other two nozzles that helped make the Sharks life miserable, Madden and Burr-dog, combined with Eags for some very productive shifts. I know I'm not the only one, don't you just love it when this line scores! Sunday, this line proved to be a lot more than 3 pretty faces. Sometimes I think the best part of Adam's game is after the whistle blows in our opponents crease. "C'mon, I dare ya; I double dog dare ya to hit me in the face!" Burr-dog's the name – agitation's the game.

Versteeg appeared a bit agitated when the Paul Bunyan that chopped his stick in two was not sentenced to two minutes. Can you imagine if that was

Thorton, Kane, Crosby or Ovechkin etc.? Somebody would have had to do time. The misunderstood Dutchie is tired of being the Rodney Dangerfield of professional hockey. To make matters worse, a few moments later he gets set up by his own teammate, serving time in the slammer for a crime he did not commit.

Compounding the situation, the entire Hawk bench was telling him to shut up when he tried to straighten the misunderstanding out. "I have feelings you know," complained the #32 car. I guess this brought out a new meaning to "taking one for the team." It reminded me of a time I was playing 16" softball and I had a full count on me with runners at 2nd and 3rd, two out. As I took my stance one of the moral supporters from the bench hollered out, "Hey Lindbloom, we've got some good hitters coming up – make sure it's a good one." That was a real vote of confidence.

Truth of the matter is, if Bolland, Ladd and the Steegernaut continue playing like they have been – the Hawks will fair quite well. Ladd has been skating his butt off, seemingly relishing the opportunities in the tough areas of the ice. Bolland seems to get better with every game – his defensive play taking a lot of bite out of the Shark attack. While this line has often times drawn the top line on the opposition, they can be extremely dangerous themselves. Speed kills, so does brute force…

Dustin Byfuglien continues to significantly impact the outcome of these games. His game winning shot was a highly intelligent play – one you would expect more from a player say of … Joe Thorton's considerable abilities. Buff could have tried to one time the puck, but was aware he didn't have to rush it. After stopping the puck, teeing it up, checking for wind direction, he took "dead aim," as Ben Hogan used to say on the links. Actually club selection could have been the difference in the game.

Buff decided to hit his five wood – Thorton tried to hammer a 300 plus yd. drive, at a crucial point in the third period, when a long iron (read wrist shot) might have sufficed. It would have looked great it if it went in, but at this point of the game a shot on net, although not as flashy, might better have served the purpose. Credit our alien in the net for making Thorton rush that incredible opportunity.

Actually in my book, Niemi was little more than adequate. (Huet would have stopped Demers shot.) When you stop 50 shots, come see me. Seriously though, the game sort of reminded me of Niemi's Last Stand, only with a happy ending. The "clawe save" on Clowe's shot was a tad short of miraculous. Our Puck Man absorbed more rubber than a drag strip.

Does anyone get the feeling that we're about to learn a lot more about Finland in the near future? So far I know they produce good vodka, oddly enough named Finlandia. From 1970 until 1990 they developed an extensive welfare state that collapsed in the 1990's. Successive governments have changed Finland's economic system through deregulation, privatization and lowering taxes.

Niemi's sudden thrust into the limelight may not only bring the Cup to its rightful home in Chi-town, he may help right our economic woes. If we have ears to hear! Think about it, if hockey took on a Socialist mindset Huet would be back in the nets because if only given the chance... oh well you know what I mean. President Obama really needs to watch a hockey game.

Marion Hossa continues to be scrutinized by the all seeing eye of Modor. Although averaging just under a point/game in the playoffs, the omniscient Chicago fan is feeling short changed. Do you want to know my take on the matter?

Think about the movie, *As Good As It Gets*. At one point Helen Hunt tells Jack Nicholson to back off, get lost and don't call me anymore. When he continues to pursue her (perhaps realizing that when a woman says no sometimes it means yes), she finally asks him something like, "Why do you want me." I guarantee you his reply melted the heart of every woman watching, "Because you make me a better man." Hossa not only continues to contribute in every intangible category there is – he makes Patrick Sharp a better player!

I'm pretty sure an elephant will forget, before the Shark fans, when it comes to Brian "abandon ship" Campbell. Their incessant boos every time Brian touches the puck are getting a tad annoying. Let it go! Breathe! Turn the other cheek. How can you boo a player who comes back about 3 weeks early from a severe clavicle injury? How about a little R-E-S-P-E-C-T?

I thought #51, the Phantom, had an outstanding game yesterday. He was a puck moving machine, weaving in and out of the shark infested waters. For the most part, the fans in Chicago have even stopped booing Brian, realizing he'll never be a Sopel. It appears they are finally appreciating him for what he brings to the table.

While on the subject of defensemen, Duncan made what I thought was one of the key plays of the game when he got caught in a moment of indecision by the Shark blue line. (Think about the Clash's song, SHOULD I STAY OR SHOULD I GO.) By the time he decided not to go after a dangling puck, Joe Thorton scooped it up and headed for pay dirt. From a standing start

Keith almost caught up with Jumbo Joe, not giving him the time needed to figure out the enigma between Chicago's pipes. Lady Luck was certainly on our side on that play, but so was an indomitable effort by our Norris Trophy candidate. By the way, when Hjarlmarrson nailed Pavelski late in the game – well there's just no other way to put this – Joey fall down, go boom.

The refereeing was one, or a combination of the following adjectives; obtuse, incongruous or flat out underhanded (seriously, 5-0 in favor of the home team?) Did Mack the Knife and his associates have a word with Watson and Devorski before the game? I'm beginning to think Brad Watson is a very bad man. Trust me; despite my cries of "kill the ref," I try to have an open mind when it comes to the zebra's.

However, when the referee said Versteeg had a guilty look on his face at the end of the game, he crossed the line. My mom will probably kill me for saying this but she once told me that her way of measuring out punishment for our miscreant ways was to whack which ever one of the 9 of us was closest. If you weren't the guilty party in that instance, no doubt you deserved it for the time you got away. It paid to be quick in the Lindbloom household!

I know I'm getting long winded, but I have to touch on one more subject. As Ricky Ricardo would say to Lucy, "Lucy, let me splain something to you." The announcers, (I thought Milbury was going to cry after the game) and even some of our beloved sports writers were quick to justifiably sing Niemi's praises. However, need I remind you we had 40 vs. the Sharks 45 shots on goal, without the benefit of a power play!

Nabokov was every bit as good as Antii, at least twice the beneficiary of the Hawks hitting the post. While Niemi contributed in a big way, it was clearly a team win. For someone to suggest that the Sharks dominated us, well they need to come up with another esplaination. I liked RoseLee's post game observation; "That was a great one to watch once the clock ran out."

She also advised me to keep doing lucky things – it's probably why my daughter's uniform is dark green this year!

5/21/10

Snug as a bug in a rug

At approximately 4:55 Tuesday afternoon, one of my co-workers hollered over to me, "Hey Lindbloom, come over and look at this!" A good friend of his, Eric, who has a toddler, found himself in quite a quandary. Rather than have me try to put it into words, I've copied the e-mail;

"Callum has been wearing red Blackhawk PJ's on game nights since the playoffs began. I think the Hawks are 5-1 when wearing said PJ's. The PJ's are getting a little snug, so I ordered a new larger pair of White Blackhawk PJ's."

Do I:

A) Squeeze him into the lucky Red PJ's for hopefully a few more weeks?

B) Switch now to the new, more comfortable Whites and risk a new streak?

C) What color Callum's PJ's are have absolutely no bearing on any NHL playoff game.

Without hesitation we all advised Eric to jam, cram or if need be, slam the kid into the red ones, periodically checking to make sure his blood and air supply are not hindered; too much. Twenty years from now the toddler we'll realize the important contribution he made when the Hawks hoisted Lord Stanley's Cup! There's a possibility Callum's PJ's could end up in the Hockey Hall of Fame. Maybe they could be raised next to the Stanley Cup banner at the United center.

Anybody besides me get the feeling it's the Hawks who are beginning to smell blood? I'm certainly not counting my chickens before there hatched, yet it seems it might take the 9th Circuit Court declaring the Sharks an endangered species to stop the Red War Party from eliminating them. That nasty old shark that chased Nemo in the Pixar movie has met his match in the diminutive, cuddly and lovable, Dave Bolland. The #36 car bears a striking resemblance to the protagonist in FINDING NEMO.

Bolland of course is the leader of the now infamous Shitz tzu Line – let me explain. While many people have seen the classic movie, ANIMAL HOUSE, I actually live in one. My loving bride has an affinity for things with four legs and fur. (Make note to self – do not invite Bennie Eager over.) In addition to our 105# Akita and 35# psychotic Wheaton Terriorist, numerous puppies and kittens have been fostered for the Humane Society over the last couple of years. Our current residents include three tiny Shitz tzu's that bring us much joy and an inexhaustible supply of fertilizer.

My son Greg will play with the gremlins, putting a blanket over himself, while letting the three curmudgeons attack. Their attack is relentless, as they claw, bite, growl and try to pull the cover off their pinned down prey. It's quite humorous to watch. They don't stop until Nathalie hollers at Greg for ruining the blanket.

Indefatigably, they go about their red work – which brings me to perhaps the main key in the Hawks playoff success so far – the Hawks third line, Ladd, Bolland and the Flying Dutchman. They bare a striking resemblance to the highly energetic fur balls. The Shitz tzu's not are very good at sharing toys which reminds me of Versteeg when he grabs hold of the puck.

When Coach Q decided to throw the Shitz tzu's against the Jumbo Joe Jerk Line, most all of us thought they were too small to be effective in containing Jaws and the boys. Like a severe case of poison ivy though, Boll's and his pack continue to get under the blanket of their adversaries. It appeared at times there were two #36 cars out on the ice. A friend noted that as was the case last year, Bolland's line has been the difference between "the thrill of victory or the agony of defeat."

Speaking of agony, make absolutely no mistake about it – Thorton tried to break Bolland's arm on the vicious, cowardly, slash just prior to the face off. So far in the playoffs our Vienna Choir Boy has now been threatened with castration by Sedin, had his head slammed into the boards by Burrows and now has reduced the great Joe Thornton into aggravated battery charges. I see a pattern developing. They once suspended Rocket Richard for the entire playoffs for similar misconduct, setting off riots in Montreal.

I read in Brian McFarlane's book, "The best of The Original Six," that Richard "pitchforked" Hal Laycoe, a former Canadian teammate, in the face which resulted in Laycoe whacking the Rocket over the head with his stick. (It should be noted that Laycoe never was penalized more than 30 min. in any season.) Richard responded by breaking a stick over the Bruin defensemen's shoulder. Finding that was not enough to assuage his discomfort, he then broke another stick over his back and then fetched a third stick. (I'm guessing you wouldn't want to be a dog in the Rocket's house.)

The reason the Rocket was eventually suspended because he punched the ref twice in the melee. I guess we should be happy that Thornton only tried to break Bolland's arm, only using one stick. Isn't it great to know we've somewhat cleaned up the game! While the devil inside of me screams, "Get that cheap shot SOB," hopefully the Hawks will wait until next season to exact just retribution.

The #16 car played like a man possessed from the opening whistle to the closing bell. When Thorton, decided to try and fight someone half his size at the end of the game, Ladd was in the thick of it. Make no mistake about it – he is the muscle on this line, quite possibly the brains. I didn't catch which player it was, but he gave one of the hammerheads a well deserved, abrasive facial. I think I enjoyed that as much as his wicked wrister in the first period.

While I'm sure all the Shark fans and announcers could have easily have snagged that heat seeking missile, it eluded a partially screened Nabokov. The Shark's blog's were calling for Nabokov's head on a platter, much like the Canuck fans blaming the great Italian goal tender. (Something tells me both will still be high picks in the Fantasy Hockey Leagues next year.) Ah fans, where would we be without them?

I know the Shark fans are bleeding teal right now. The fans in the Tank are as passionate as any I've seen – my heart goes out to you, I feel your pain.

(But I'm really glad it's your pain!) Before picking up those stones though, realize with a bounce here of deflection there, the Sharks could be at least 1-1 in this series. When Vancouver was in town for The Mother's Day Massacre, there was a young man and lady sitting about 6 seats over from us in Sec 320, row 10 in Canuck garb. As the Hawks took a shellacking that night, I observed this young couple trying to conceal their obvious joy.

What is it about hockey that will take us fan-attics to a city 2,000 miles away to exhort on our warriors? Late in the third while a few of us were getting ready to jump, that couple was smiling and singing along to a Beatles song. I envied their happiness, feeling somewhat humiliated by the outcome of the game. You just know that couple had PJ's, or at the very least fancy underwear, with goofy looking Orca's on them. Unfortunately for them, they were singing "Yesterday" a few days later.

Hossa, who is somewhat familiar with that song, has been skating under the radar throughout the playoffs. Could the third time be the charm? I say under the radar because I don't think his significant contributions are noticed by the intelligentsia who think he should be an Ovechkin or Crosby. (Wait a minute bad comparison, those guys are not playing at the moment.) His play setting up Brouwer's goal is what makes him perhaps one of the top 10 players in the league. His defense and hockey intelligence in the playoffs has played a significant part in our forward advance into enemy territory. If you still think he isn't contributing enough for what he's being compensated, close your eyes and try imagining the Hawks without him. I'm pretty sure that movie would be called "Nightmare on Madison Street."

Once again we got a great effort from the Cruiser Bruiser Line. Eager continues to hammer away at the color teal like he wants to destroy it. What I've really noticed about #55 is the speed he's skating with out there. Burr-dog, obviously more of a pit bull than Shitz tzu, even drew a penalty while striving to reestablish order in front of the Shark crease. When this line can cause the other team's hooligans to go to the time out box, it bodes well for our men in red. Although Hawk fans are well aware that this line just ain't right, it never hurts to have some "excitable boys" out there. As Nurse Ratchet might put it, "Time for your medicine boys."

I'm not sure what drug Niemi is taking, but he certainly has been cool as a cucumber. It took a twisted wrister off of Marleau's stick, to finally dent the net. I think he had all of a 6"x 6" spot to hit in the upper corner. Like that caveman who rams the Zamboni into the half boards, I believe he yelled, "Bullseye!" Ring the bell on that shot. In what's known in the sales world as beating the bushes, one great big atta-boy to Dale Tallon, for finding the Finnish Phenom in some obscure rink in Fantaa, Finland.

I'm pretty sure the intensity level will be ratcheted up another notch on Friday. Callum, hate to do this to you, but it's time to man up. Put on those PJ's. Suck it in big boy! Eric, if necessary, cut some holes in the footsies. Go get em, Shitz tzu's.

While I was pecking away at the computer guess who just called. Despite the bitter protests of my daughter, Nathalie just took in a young feline whose eyes are swollen shut – that kitty kat will be purring like a kitten in no time. I think were going to name her Stanley, for obvious reasons. It appears I married a distant offspring of St. Francis of Assissi.

5/28/10

The Few, The Proud, The Committed

It all happens at such incredible speed in the NHL; be advised, don't blink an eye. The Tribune has done a tremendous job capturing the euphoria of the fans reactions to those moments in pictures. I love studying them, looking at all the ecstatic expressions as fans celebrate that moment when the puck crosses the goal line.

Last Saturday, May 22 on page 3 of the sports section, Tribune photographer Scott Strazzante captured a fleeting moment – a moment before the moment so to speak. Big Buff is skating away in exaltation a nanosecond after his lethal Darth Maul laser. A stunned Nabokov appears to be in a state of disbelief. However, truly the heart of the picture is on the other side of the plexi-glass, that thin barrier that separates us from our red clad warriors.

The puck has already hit the roof of the net, yet it appears that only about 6 people in the crowd at this point have realized what has just happened. A man in a white shirt gets it – he's already signaling for a touch down! The girl two rows directly below him is in the incipient stages of a Mt. St. Helen's eruption. The guy in row 3 about 4 seats over seems to be saying, "Did I just see what I thought I saw? Another girl, with a white Hossa sweater, two seats in from the stairs about row 7 is clearly ahead of the curve!

The player largely responsible for the pandemonium that is a moment away is largely hidden by a stunned Douglas Murray. (On the bright side, Murray won't have to miss any more hair styling appointments.) Look closely to Murray's right, you can make out a 36 on the left arm of the player affectionately known as The Rat. David Bolland's nickname is about to be changed with a new surname, one that involves a coronation – KING DAVID.

Clearly, the Bible is thought by many as a boring anachronism of questionable Jewish history. No doubt, as Charles Spurgeon once noted, "there is enough dust on most of your bibles to write the word damnation." Yet when one actually takes time to study it, it is a fascinating book, an interwoven tapestry of stories and events that repeat themselves century after century.

One of my favorite stories is about a little Sheppard boy and a Philistine giant named Goliath. Some 3,035 years after the original event, I believe we just witnessed a reenactment of that, the cards are stacked against you, epic bout. If it's possible, the odds of David triumphing against the nasty Philistine were less than the Cubs winning the World Series.

1 Sam 17:4-7, states that Goliath was over 9 feet tall. For 40 days he mocked the Israelites – taunting then to send a brave man to settle things once and for all. When Thornton, err I mean Goliath saw David, he bellowed, "Am I a dog that you come at me with sticks?" David's reply is one of my favorite in the entire Bible; "You come at me with sword and spear and javelin, but I come against you in the name of the Lord Almighty the God of the armies of Israel, whom you have defied." I still get shivers down my spine when I read that verse.

You would have to be brain dead not to see the comparison between that Bible story, Bolland and Jumbo Joe Thornton. While I'll admit, much like Adam and Eve, Thornton was a bit snake bitten, he was lucky to leave town with his head still attached to his torso. When Bolland was not singled out for bogus penalties, (goalie interference and when Pavelski held his arm), he and his line mate's plagued the desperate Sharks. It almost seemed the referee's were told by NHL officials, "Look, we don't want Dave Bolland to be the face of the NHL." At one point, as this line skated around the ice like a starved school of piranha, the TV announcer said, "Ye gad. This is their third line!!"

Bolland's goal in Game 3 was electrifying. It came moments after the Hawks had killed off his only legitimate penalty. While the raucous fans were still standing in appreciation for the kill, Jonny on the spot blocked a shot and our little Sheppard boy was off to the races. His Herculean effort was almost thwarted by Nabokov – who clearly deserved a better fate that night. Davy had all of 2" to slide the puck past their beleaguered net minder.

The fans gladly remained standing, actually some started jumping up and down and hugging each other. Their "breathing easy" period lasted all of about two minutes. Marleau, who was superb in all four games, crosschecked Campbell out of the way before tallying his second goal of the game; so much for gliding into the finish line. Make no mistake about it though, when the #36 car was asked to **Commit to the Indian** he said, "Fetch my sling and five smooth stones." Can you say timber!

While on the subject of Lilliputians, for those of you who read the "Snug as a Bug in a Rug" piece – yes Callum sucked it in and wore the lucky PJ's. After the game I texted Callum's dad, Eric, and said, "Friday's game was the type of effort that would enrich the coffers of the local drinking establishments into the wee hours of the morning when I was younger."

Eric replied, "You are spot on, on the post party after a game like that – we would have been doing cannonballs in the Chicago River back in '91."

When Moehawk, (a grade school friend who now lives in Dallas but still has the Indian Head firmly implanted in her heart), heard about Callum her response epitomized the essence of those women who love the red clad warriors. "After reading about Callum outgrowing his PJ's, my first reaction was to cut the feet, arms, crotch and anything else that doesn't fit. The game is tonight – he'd better be wearing them." There's just something about a woman who wears RED! When Callum was asked to **Commit to the Indian,** he mumbled "Goo goo, ga ga, da da!" – roughly translated – Game on. Let's do this thing, dad!

I guess I could shorten this treatise and give you the Cliff Notes version of Games 3 and 4 – Big Buff, the new screen saver on my daughter's computer, tallies game winner on Friday and again on Sunday. However words tend to fly out of my distorted mind like flowers scattered in a mountain meadow, as the saying goes, "strewn forth like babbling idiots." Basically, Buff Dusted them off and Davy Bowled them over. Bolland's quote on his assist on the #33 cars back breaker Friday was dead on. "Buff was yelling for the puck and he's pretty hard to miss out there!" You might say he's the proverbial bull in a China shop.

King David's feather touch pass to big boy was as my son would put it – "Sa-weet!" Dustin's roofer was merely the icing on the cake. One of the announcers on TV was wondering how the Sharks could leave the behemoth so wide open. It's elementary my dear Watson; when you have Toews and Kane on the same line, you pay a little less attention to the lesser of three evils. And make no mistake about it – when the puck is on Patrick's stick, evil is a good description if you're the opponent.

Actually, in addition to his butt in the face of the goalie game winner on Sunday, the Buffanator had two consecutive huge hits. Two suicidal Sharks decided to take a run at the Mack truck on skates. Look, I'm no genius, but when a Prius collides with a Ford F150, the truck wins, every time. After the second Shark, (who also became airborne), took a run at Buff in retribution for his buddy who was still dusting off his shorts, Dustin yelled, "NEXT!" It was like watching a Chuck Norris movie. When Big Buff was asked to **Commit to the Indian,** Sharks began to fly.

Speaking of burly men with red sweaters, (the Michael Flatley impersonator in Sec. 116), we now have a clear cut winner in this years Dancing With the Hawks contest. (John Travolta got nothing on this enormous man with happy feet!) Two weeks ago after a game, I e-mailed the Hawks Senior Customer Service Executive Aaron Salsbury to find out what the name of the song was he danced to. Despite constantly hounding me for mo and mo money, Aaron's been of great assistance throughout the season.

I wanted to mention Burly Man in one of these pieces as a tribute to the fans who are doing the little things to make this season so memorable. Aaron responded, "The song is called Shipping Out to Boston and it nauseates me. They play it at almost any Boston sporting event." However, even Aaron admitted the big guy brought out his A-game on Sunday. When the Caucasian Byfuglien impersonator was asked to **Commit to the Indian,** he put on those blue suede shoes!

I thought about joining in as my feet have been known to get happy while listening to that banjo and fiddle crap. The only thing stopping me was the memory of one of the contestants of American Idol a few years back. After his performance, Simon turned him every which way but loose. "An atrocious song choice, sung in the pitch of geese farts on a muggy afternoon (thank you Leo Kottke) and by the way – the dancing was hideous!"

The comment about the dancing stung a little because it was almost a mirror image of my best moves. Eh, critics – what do they know anyway. They told Jethro Tull a flute would never make it in a Rock and Roll band. They told Ray Kroc a fast food business would never make it. When I was asked to **Commit to the Indian,** Doc Watson's version of "Hold the Woodpile Down," got my feet a tapping.

Went to a party the other night – hold the wood pile down
everything wrong and nothing was right – hold the wood pile down
I saw my gal, we snuck out the back – hold the wood pile down
I kissed her once, she said "Here comes my dad! – hold the wood pile down.

We have a player who has held the woodpile down the entire playoffs, yet remains an underachiever in many Hawk fans minds. While it was recently pointed out to me that "there are liars, damn liars and statistics," numbers do help paint a picture. (How do you measure hustle or desire?) The #81 car, who I thought was the best player on the ice on Sunday, is tied for the lead in +/- at +8. The Corsi Rating which I've finally figured out, I think, is a great stat to keep in mind. It measures the shots attempted for a team vs. how many are attempted against while a given player is on the ice, per 60 minutes. Hossa's +25.7 rating is second on the team only to Kopecky..

It hurts my head to much to think about the Qualcomp, Qual team, TOI/60, GFON/60 etc. but suffice it to say Hossa leads the team with a 2.02 rating. In other words, he's one of the Hawks best players! When Hossa was asked to **Commit to the Indian,** he said "Show me the money!" Just kidding, he actually said "When the puck is on the ice, the #81 car will be in the vicinity." I'm pretty sure he also stated that "the third time is the charm."

In his on the ice post game interview with Goldilocks on Sunday, Toews made a salient point. "Everyone's contributing, whether they play 20 minutes or 5 minutes. The #55 car has been motoring around the rink like an accident waiting to happen. When Big Ben hit Couture in the first period, you could read the agitated Shark's forward's lips as he dusted himself off, "You a_ _ hole." Bet he had his head up next time Eager jumped over the boards, "Cruising for a Bruising," as they say.

Actually, Bolland on his game tying tally deflected praise to Eager for his hard work along the boards. I did mention to a friend that it might not be a good idea to throw #55 out on the ice late in the third period – he actually might have gotten away with a "Wooly Bully" elbow early in the third. How do you try and tell the # 55 car to take his foot off the accelerator a little? When Big Ben was asked to **Commit to the Indian,** he said, "It's clobbering time!"

Jordan Hendry took a few lumps for the team, as usual. Last year, #6 was skating for the Ice Hogs. This year he's finding himself trying to corral some of the fastest studs in the NHL. It appears that he has been cautioned to not pinch in much in the O-zone. Actually, during the last two games, that seemed to be the Hawks modus operandi to me. Odd man rushes were few and far between for the Sharks, quite a contrast to the Predator series. Hendry, got the short end of the stick when he became entangled with Jumbo Joe in the first period. After being treated like an altar boy in the Boston Archdiocese, Hendry became the victim of Blind Justice.

When he was sent to the box I had smoke coming out of my ears. It reminded me of a time this year when I had ordered a Honkers Ale. There was a lady, probably around 60, who started pouring the nectar when I said, "Can you leave it in the bottle. I want to throw it at the referee when I'm finished." With a sparkle in her eye, she motioned like she was going to give me two empty bottles. Apparently, this damsel had seen enough of her share of bad calls against Chicago teams to empathize with me. Her beguiling smile brought a moment of joy to my heart. When the Honkers lady was asked to **Commit to the Indian,** she did not hesitate to make sure the good guys had some arrows in their quivers!

Geronimo, aka Jonathan Toews, continues his stellar post season play. If it's possible to relax at all during the playoffs, the best chance for that is when #19 hops over the boards. If Bolland is a Shitz tzu, Jonathon is a Doberman. Two words describe Toews in my mind; dogged determination. While standing in line in the Men's room between the 2nd and 3rd periods, the guy in front of me whispered, "If we win today, we'll be taking home some hardware." While talking in the bathroom is a major violation of the rules of Men's room etiquette, I had to ask him what he was talking about. (Real men do not chat in the bathroom. They concentrate on the matter at hand.) He whispered, "The Campbell Conference trophy."

Trying not to jinx that possibility, I didn't tell any of the three people I was with until Steeger slid one in the empty net. While Toews did not hoist the trophy, he did manage to pick up a few of Duncan Keith's teeth that were still littering the ice. When Toews was asked to **Commit to the Indian,** he said "I'll lead by example, every second of every shift."

The # 2 car downplayed coming back for the 3rd period after almost swallowing what he must have thought was a moon pie. Duncan Keith told a reporter, "It's really not as big a deal as everyone thinks." Duncan clearly has a new understanding of that old saying, "This steak tastes like rubber." His teammates were laughing when he sounded like that old Batman character, Mumbles. Go ahead; try to say any word with a T or Th in it without your front teeth. Do you think you could pronounce Norris Trophy without your two front teeth? I think you'd get stuck on the "phy" part. I have a crazy idea. To prove to Duncan that there is a Tooth Fairy, let's all mail in $1 to the following address to show our appreciation; (I'm serious, dead serious.)

Chicago Blackhawks
Attn: Duncan Keith
1904 West Madison Ave.
Chicago, Il. 60612

When Duncan Keith was asked to **Commit to the Indian,** he said, "I regret that I have but seven teeth to give to my team."

Could it be possible that Finland is a front for Antti Niemi – aka Atom Antti? I'm beginning to think he's an Android. If you were to dissect his brain encasing, you would find a lot of wires, and circuit boards and crap. Although it could have been steam, I thought I detected smoke coming from his ears after a couple of the scrambles in front of his net. He could be from another planet, because his play has clearly been out of this world.

Remember when all the pundits didn't think the Hawks had the goaltending for a shot at the Cup? I'm reminded of that Blondie song "And you don't stop and you can't stop and you just keep eating pucks." When the #31 car was asked to **Commit to the Indian,** he said in a fake Finnish accent, "I do not understand what they are saying about shaky goal tending – It Does Not Compute!!"

Our other defenseman, Campbell, Hjarlmarrson, Seabs and Mr. GQ himself – Brent Sopel, have been the difference in my opinion in two out of the three playoff series. (I still think the tandem of Weber and Suter was as good as anyone we faced. It's a good deal of the reason we struggled so with those tenacious Predators.) All you fans who have bemoaned Soupy's defensive play this year – admit it, your ecstatic he's back. I'm sort of thinking Sope's knows what it takes to win. Seabs is tied for the lead, +8, in the plus minus category. Hjarlmarrson could be a Norris candidate someday if he picks up the offense a bit. For now I'll settle for his shutdown defense. When these guys were asked to **Commit to the Indian,** they said, "The crease is my turf; I spit on your slap shot."

If you are still reading at this point, you really need to get a life. One last tidbit; about 7 weeks ago now, my son made two wooden plaques in his wood shop class with hockey teams names on them. They were the Blackhawk's and the Flyers. He only painted one of them though – the Blackhawk's one. We may have a celebratory burning of the Flyer plaque before Saturday's tussle. As we drove together to the Game last Sunday Greg said, "Dad, look." There was a huge Hawk circling above us at a stop light. "I think it's a good omen," he said. It reminded me of one of my favorite Hawks of all time – When Denis Savard was asked to **Commit to the Indian ...** well I guess that's why #18 is hanging in the rafters.

Stay committed Callum, just two more weeks - hold the wood pile down,

6/4/10

122

Queen Pawn Opening's – a walk on the wild side

Yes Mr. McCartney, it is a long and winding road – but hockey in June? While coming close to resembling a bowling league in length, at least the hockey season will eventually draw to a close. As the saying goes for those of us sitting in the nose bleeds, "There are two seasons – the hockey season itself and waiting for the hockey season to begin." With the Hawks apprehensively holding a 2-1 series lead at the moment against the Orange men from Syracuse, err I mean Philadelphia, it appears we're about to enter the second season. My guess is that this season will extend a few more games then we would like!

Admit it; you wanted this series to be easy on you - a 4-1 sleeper where we could bask in the glow of the warm fuzzies that emanated from the first three series. No doubt a few of you threw in a couple of Muhammad Ali's "I am the greatest," boasts. Many thought this would be a 4 to 5 game dispatch of the 7th seed in the "weaker" Eastern Conference. A friend at work verbalized what a lot of fans were thinking, "Get your ticket for the parade right now!"

"Not so fast," said a speedy and talented team from Philly. The Flyer who has caught my eye the most is a 22 year old who is about to put in for a big raise. Claude Giroux reminds of the Road Runner that Wily Coyote could never successfully track down. I believe his skates could melt ice the way is flying around the pond. Gagne, Carter, Richards (will someone please punch that nozzle in the face), Jay Leno, Hartnell, Timonen and the uglier version of Lerch of the Adam's family - #20, are a lot to keep track of.

Actually, the key to stopping Hartnell may be found in the Bible. The story of Samson and Delilah comes to mind. When the two timing tramp found out the secret to his strength, she cut Samson's pristine hair thus breaking the Levite oath, rendering him powerless to fight off the Philistines. I'm not sure if cutting off Hartnell's flowing locks will slow him down – but it would vastly improve the hirsute wingers look. He's beginning to pose a striking resemblance to Hagrid from Harry Potter. Where's the hair pulling Alexandre Burrows when you really need him?

During Wednesday's loss, I found myself on more than one occasion saying, "the Flyer's are out skating us." Their explosive offense reminded me of a time in my son's toddler days. We were flying out to Seattle which takes roughly four hours. Greg had not pooped in a week – but we came prepared with four diapers, just in case. About 1 hour into the flight, explosion #1 occurred. (Now a days Greg would be considered a terrorist.) After the second explosion, the stewardess asked everyone in the back of the plane if they wanted to be relocated; it stunketh!

Only one gentleman got up and moved as far west on the plane as he could. To make a long story short, after we went through all four of our diapers, we luckily borrowed one from another mom on the plane. By the time we disembarked, that diaper was full to the brim so to speak! Nathalie's mom and dad were smiling at us in the terminal as we approached them, but not for long. We handed Greg to his grandpa, who held him at arms length and exclaimed, "Son, you are ripe!"

I can't help but connect this memory to something the RoseLee told me after the vicissitudes of Game One. She asked me if one of the unsung hero's of these playoffs, one year old Callum, continues to be stuffed into his overgrown, lucky red Blackhawk pajamas. "If Callum was wearing his pajama's last night and watching the game and understanding what was going on, the pajama's might not be fit for wear anymore. I would not be surprised if the same condition was present in half of the fandom that night." To borrow a line from the movie *The Nutty Professor,* "You done made me mess my pants."

Actually the diverse natures of Games 1 and 2 reminded me of a chess match. Chess, despite all its time consuming thinking, is an explosive game. It's so much better than X-box or Play station at raising the heartbeat. If you ever played the game, at least at my amateurish level, no two games ever come close to resembling each other. In my mind, this series thus far has been a snapshot of the exciting conclusion to the movie, *In Search of Bobby Fisher.* If you haven't seen that movie rent it. It is the chess version of the movie, *Miracle on Ice.*

In the movie, the young boy is torn between a sound conservative strategy or boldly taking the offensive. True to form, the Flyers remain an "offensive" team. I've always favored Queen Pawn openings over the mirror image, defensive minded King pawn starts. Moving the Queen Pawn out often leads to a highly erratic, discombobulated battlefield. This in turn causes much anxiety but considerably more excitement. The Flyer's have definitely been playing with a Queen Pawn mindset. But then again what would you expect from a bunch of queens?

Actually, the various pieces on the chessboard resemble the different abilities of a hockey team. The pieces all have different strengths, weaknesses and strategies. In hockey, the goaltenders are clearly the Kings. They don't move much, but you can't win without them. Even the lowliest piece on the board, the pawn, can stifle the powerful attack of the

Killer Queen bee. The Flyers decided to place a powerful rook, Carcillo, in favor of a bishop, van Riemsdyk, in an attempt to add a little brute force in Game 2.

Predictably, the game immediately turned into an antagonistic affair. The evil spirit that was driven from Wild Man of Gerasenes, (see Mark 5), seems to have found a new home in Carcillo. He was in the top five in penalties this year, logging over 200 minutes in the time out box. (I still haven't forgiven Don Blocker for picking him up during the playoffs of our Fantasy league this year in order to win the penalty minute category. It gave me an indication of the type of player Blocker is!)

Carcillo has spent over 4 hours this year in the time out box, quietly reflecting on the evils of his ways. That was a "tad" short of the all-time NHL season record of 472 minutes! That total was amassed by another Philly thug known as Dave "The Hammer" Schultz. "The Hammer" combined with Bob "The Hound" Kelly to terrorize opponents with a style of play that more closely resembled aggravated battery than hockey. The ref's were given hazardous duty pay when they officiated a Flyer slugfest. Think of the Hound and the Hammer as Cam Janssen's on steroids. Carcillo, who played most of the evening like a derailed train, appears to be a student of the old time, fisticuff filled Flyer hockey.

When you think of the Flyers, and Philadelphia in general, the word toughness comes to mind. Actually a lot of words come to mind, most unprintable. While in line at a cash machine last Monday, I struck up a conversation with a man who had some friends heading to Wednesdays tussle in the City of Brotherly Love. (Now that's an oxymoron for you!) "They won't be wearing their Hawk jerseys though," he admitted. Like their hockey team, Flyer fans do not play well with others.

They remind me of a moment during a Bear game in December several years ago against the Buffalo Bills. We were freezing our frozen tundra's off with temperatures hovering in the teens. A total nutcase who was built like a Greek God and dressed in nothing but a loin cloth, had his entire body painted and was taunting Bear fans as he completely circled Soldiers Field half naked.

I know I was not the only Bear fan thinking, "Someone (else) needs to kick his ass." In one of the most shameful moments in Chicago sport fans history, all we did was boo the bum. In Philadelphia, someone would have died that day! Hell, they tried to take out Santa Claus with snowballs one time. John Madden was quoted as saying, "The Chicago players on the ice are safer than the Blackhawk fans in the stands in Philly." Given a choice, Flyer fans would rather sign Carcillo than Giroux.

For one reason or another, the Flyers tried to take out Kopecks in Game 2. The # 82 car is making a strong case for himself, filling in for the banged up #16 car who remains in the repair shop. One of the best players on the ice for the Hawks in Game 1, Tomas continues to make his presence felt. Carcillo and Pronger specifically made it known that Kopecks needed to be punished, although I'm not sure why.

Much like that commercial where the car is being chased by the demonic snowmen, Tomas avoided becoming a pancake when Carcillo and Carter decided to tag team him. In what has turned out to be one of the greatest collisions in the Playoffs, the # 13 car for the Flyers totaled the #17 car on his own team, when Kopecks slammed on his breaks. I'm actually a little surprised one of the Flyers enforcers didn't take a run at Carcillo for that hit! Burr-dog had to add his two cents hollering from the Hawks bench repeatedly, "that was your best hit this year!"

Kopecky's contributions remind me of three other Hawks who are relegated to the sidelines at the moment. All of them contributed significantly to the Hawks fortunes in this magical season. I say magical because as Callum's dad, Eric, noted "When freaking Kopecky and Eager both have game winners in the Finals ... you know these guys must have been sprinkled with fairy dust."

Colin Fraser has always been a favorite of mine. Although not quite in the despised Bobby Clarke league talent wise, Colin reminds me of the nozzle I most wanted to see get pummeled in the 70's. (Bobby Clarke made Adam Burrish look like a choir boy.)The #46's cars commitment to the Indian has never been in doubt and I never saw him give less than 100% on any shift. More than likely he'll take a run at Pronger on his first shift. "Tall doesn't scare me," bellowed Colin.

Is it just me, or do some of you miss the boyish face of Cam Barker patrolling our blue line. When you see a player come up through the organization, you tend to think of them as family. Admittedly, he would make an occasional bonehead play at times in the d-zone. Yet, tell me you don't miss #25 out there on the point during our power plays. I recall him sticking up for Patrick Kane on more than one occasion when someone would try to send #88 a message. Although I recall the opposition scoring as Barker sat in the box for being "the third man in", you can't let the hooligans on the other team take runs at your diminutive teammates. It's not hard for me to hope Cam does well with the Wild.

Lastly, the enigma that is Cristobal Huet continues to prepare and stay focused if, God forbid at this moment, the need should arise. In my mind, the brass nuts of the goal tending controversy have been Antti's incredible play, more so than Huet's ineptitude. Meanwhile, Cristobal remains the only athlete in Chicago history more maligned than Milton Bradley or Rex Grossman. While at some point in the season management made a wise decision to ride #31 to the Finnish line, keep your head up Cristobal, no one knows what the future holds. One of the highlights of the season for me was when Huet stopped 12 out of 13 Blue Jackets in a shoot out. I also got excited when he flattened Janssen in his crease! Even the people who wanted him guillotined cheered him that night!

In the movie OCEAN'S 11, one of the greatest heists of all time takes place, when an impregnable Vegas Casino experiences a major withdrawal. Niemi's effort in Game 2 eclipsed that grand theft. Dan McNeil of the Tribune wrote one of the best lines on hockey I've read all year after Game one – "Hockey forever has been about team." I totally agree but in Game two, especially for the last 30 minutes of play, Blackhawk hockey was about Antti Niemi. He almost blocked as many shots as Brent Sopel!

During my youthful days I often heard the refrain from my dad, "What do I have to do to get through to you?" I'm sure the Flyers were thinking, "What do we have to do to get one through the Finnish Phenom." The extended ovation for "Mr. Not in My Kitchen," was thunderous after the game ended. I've seen quite a few big moments in the last 45 years at the Stadium and United Center. However, I can't recall, (maybe Jordan), an ovation like the one the #31 car got when he was named number one star of the game.

Sarah Kustok, in one of her more brilliant interviews, was about to start speaking when she realized no one would be able to hear a word she said. Goldilocks then, in one of those special moments, clapped her hands towards Niemi and then held the microphone up towards the 300 Level. If it were possible, it seemed the decibel level shot up another 20 points. While that explosion of sound known as Motown will never be surpassed in my mind, the ovation for Antti came pretty close. Niemi just leaned on the boards, exhausted, and was probably doing one of three things;

1. Just basking in the glow of his brilliant performance or...

2. Trying to figure out what the heck to say and how to say it in English.

3. Wondering where the horse shoe that fell out of his bloomers was.

In any language that night his play spoke for itself – "The Puck Stops Here."

I do have to mention my son Greg's brilliant observation on the game winning goal by Eager in Game 2. Leighton's glove was leight on that shot. (You're killing me Greg!) Not to be outdone I countered, "Niemi's glove save on Asham's laser in the second period was fin-nomenal." Greg and I tend to crack each other up.

Was it just me, or did anyone else seem to notice the lack of penalties called during Game 3. How is it that Hartnell can take a fist to the back of Versteeg's head, knocking his helmet off, and skate away with impunity? Who does he think he is, Pronger? Also after getting mauled by Pronger, including a vicious cross check to Buff's lower back, the zebra's assess a penalty to Dustin? I'm beginning to think there is a racial thing going on here.

Where are Al Sharpton and Jesse Jackson when you need them. While "Operation Push" may be a good program for the cities youth – I thought it was a penalty in hockey, not a defensive strategy. The Flyers, until this series, were averaging just less than 6 penalties per game in the playoffs; against the Hawks, that average has shrunk to about two per game. Could it really be true that the Kings of malfeasance and thuggery have cleaned up their act? Could the ghost of the Hound and the Hammer finally be laid to rest; highly doubtful! Obviously, "hear no evil, see no evil and speak no evil" may be a good thing to teach our children – it is not a good strategy while officiating a hockey game.

Well it's Thursday afternoon and it's time to draw a conclusion to this dissertation. We now hold a precarious 2-1 lead. While trying to protect this tenuous advantage, what style of game do you think Friday night will bring about? Will the Hawks use the Queen Pawn opening or play Predator hockey? In the dark recesses of my mind, a nightmare reoccurs where the Flyers come out in orange Cooperalls. Could you imagine looking at Hartnell or Carcillo in padded tights? (Scary!)

As we head into Friday's battle, I'm reminded of what my friend Jerry McPartlin recently told me. You're not playing for the Stanley Cup until you win your third game. Hopefully we'll be vying for the Cup on Sunday. Although my antipathy for Pronger has grown in leaps and bounds during the first three games, he did say something that I could really appreciate. When he was asked by a reporter after the Canadian series if he was surprised how easy the victory was in game 4, he spoke with the wisdom of a wily veteran, "By no stretch of the imagination have any of these playoff games been easy." Expect nothing less as we try to eke out two more wins this season.

For those of you who have seen IN SEARCH OF BOBBY FISHER, you'll no what I mean when I say it's time to "move the Queen out!"

6/7/10

Demon in Disguise

Dave Bolland's countenance in the picture by Nuccio Dinuzzo on May 24th in the Tribunes sport section, somewhat unnerved me when I first gazed at it. It reminded me of an old David Bromberg album, called *"Demon in Disguise"* (albums are those big pizza shaped discs stored in the attic). Take a good look at the # 36 car in this photo. If you painted two pointy ears on him, wouldn't he resemble a Faustian devil? Now I'm aware Hawk fans think of Bollsy as an altar boy; yet maybe he's not quite as angelic as we think. Perhaps he is a closet Burr-dog.

Recently, I just "got" the joke that explained how Bolland got Sedin so mad he turned into a Carcillo. Apparently, Dave told Sedin that his brother was ugly. (It took me a few days to get it, until I finally realized the Sedin's are identical twins.) I'm still laughing about that one.

Although the accusations are probably unfounded, I do intend to keep a closer eye on #36 to see if the "little devil" moniker fits our Vienna Choir Boy. Lately, when his line takes the ice, they manage to find a little "**Sugar in the Gourd**." Like the mandolin in that song, the Shitz tzu line was smoking in game 5. In order to save the other lines, Quenneville decided to split the original Shitz tzu's up – a kind of spread the wealth mind set. Why should only one line get to have Laddie on it! Adding Big Buff to this line proved to be catastrophic for the Flyers; Bolland - a goal and an assist, Buff – two goals, two assists, Versteeg – a goal, two assists and a limo.

To back up for a second, this Bolland led line was named after the three Shitz tzu's we've been fostering for the Humane Society. One of the original members of that line was adopted. However my wife quickly replaced it with a tiny kitten named Rainy who was at the time blinded by a virus and very anemic. If an animal needs love to make it healthy, they come to the right spot when Nathalie starts to care for them.

A minor miracle seems to have taken place during the Cup Finals. Rainy can now see out of one eye and apparently thinks she's a dog. The other day I took a picture of them all sleeping together – Rainy lying on top of Buster. Of course, Greg and Nathalie now want to adopt her. I made a deal with them – if the Hawks win the Cup we keep her and change her name permanently to "Stanley!"

Although no one would ever mistake Buff for Stanley, Dustin probably played the best game of his career in a Hawk uniform. His play reminded me of The Jesus and Mary Chain song called, "**Head On.**" That song contains a lead that at the end that ranks in my top 3 all time guitar leads.

The first time I heard the song I was on my way to Toledo with a co-worker on a gray Monday morning. Did you ever hear a song for the first time and immediately replay it 5 times in a row, with increasing volume each time? (That could help explain why I now wear hearing aids.) The third time we played that song a very irate cop in an unmarked Mustang, (that Billy almost ran off the road when the officer startled us), angrily motioned for us to pull it over.

I'm pretty sure Pronger wished someone had pulled the # 33 car over in Game 5. Think Mack Truck on skates heading out of control, downhill in the Rockies, with the brakes beginning to smoke. Then try to visualize Pronger being turned into Buff's personal speed ramp. If Dustin had not scored a point in game 5, he would have been my choice for #1 star of the game based on his 9 hits These 9 hits were not bumps, or light hearted finishing of checks. They were major collisions that usually left someone singing London Bridges.

Any thing in his way was hit – **Head On.** Pronger was reduced to nothing more than Dustin's personal boy toy. In fact, if I remember nothing else about this incredible season, I'll never forget Pronger flying into the boards. It was the play of the year in my book. I think 22,300 fans jumped to their feet in triumphant unison when Pronger was dismissed! The hit in the third period, when Buff simultaneously plastered Timonen and O'Halloran, was better than the hit Carcillo put on Carter!

Versteeg, who has a little Curly Neal of the Harlem Globetrotter's in him, made a move along the left half boards that left three Flyers scratching their heads. I think they were thinking, "Is Houdini on the Hawks?" I was screaming, "Dump it deep, when somehow, defying all odds, he emerged with the puck in a dangerous area of the Flyer zone. As Sam Fels noted, Kris can go "Country stupid" at times, yet I truly enjoy watching our lovable puck hog. Versteeg has more moves than a Soul Train dancer. Keep throwing it down Kris!! My friend Don, after Versteeg's goal, earnestly stated "We need to keep him next year."☹

David Haugh of the Tribune wrote one of those lines after Game 5 that succinctly described the battle in a nutshell, "But it was the home team's style of play as they attacked with an urgency even the most casual of hockey fan **"felt."** As that old saying goes, "He didn't like emotion because he felt, but because he felt deeply." I've always tended to follow the Hawks with my heart – obviously it's been broken a few times. Yet, as that country singer croons, "This is my Country, these are my people…"

With each highlight reel goal, rugby scrum in front of Antti–matter, bone jarring hit or totally bogus penalty called on us, I felt what was transpiring "on frozen pond." I rocked back and forth in my chair trying to avoid a hit, then jump up with hands lifted high and exalted when we tickle the twine. When the brain dead referee incorrectly singles out one of our lads for a phantom infraction of the rules, my immediate response is to go over the last 4 penalties he let Pronger go unpunished for.

The feeling after our opponents score is one of the worst in sports. Jeff Tay, of the great Hockey Fantasy web site, dailyfaceoff.com, wrote to me that it gets "eerily quiet' in the United Center when we're scored upon. He suggested I try to start a cheer at that point, but as Jim Croce sang "that's not the way it feels."

Do any of you wrestling with the emotion this game evokes want to strangle an NBC announcer that apparently takes sides with the opposition? What a complete imbeciles. How dare they say the Hawks have been outplayed by the Flyers, despite what the stats indicate! The mother hen syndrome is quite prevalent in hockey fans. It's hard to be a casual observer of this game once you get "hooked" by the larceny laced mayhem taking place on the ice.

I did feel the line changes Coach Q made were almost another Faustian pact with the devil. I'm wondering if the Shitz tzu's should be tossed out there against Briere's line in Game 6. Despite suspected mass murderer, Chris Pronger, apparently already being coronated for the series MVP, Briere is the Flyer who is causing sleepless nights in Chi-town. He's been as Old Man Potter in the movie *It's a Wonderful Life* would put it, "A thorn in our side for too long."

Against the Hawks, Briere has 9 points and is a +3. With about five minutes to play in the third as the lines skated off for a shift change, Duncan Keith tapped Briere on the pads. I didn't see what happened next, but I think the # 2 car was apologizing for the high stick that will probably leave Daniel with a colorful eye for game 6. Whether or not Keith wins the Norris, I'm so glad he skates for the Hawks – what a class act.

Keith's partner, whose Indian name means "little brook running into big sea," would have had the Atomic Fireball hit of the game if it wasn't for Buff's bunker buster on Pronger. Late in the third period, in a wild scrum in front of Niemi's net, Brent, justifiably in my mind, gave Richards a hard right to the chops. Now that's hockey! It came after a furious attempt to loosen the puck from Niemi's grasp by Richards. I'm pretty sure if the #18 car wore the Indian on his chest I could appreciate his biting, clawing, hair pulling, scratching and whatever it takes attitude. For now though, we need to send the Flyers bad boy a stern message; not that he'd get it.

Several of the sportswriters are doing great job of covering these playoffs. Admit it Hawkheads, even if you don't agree with them, it's nice to see the extended coverage. Remember when we were relegated to page 8? One area I question in recent columns though is how anyone could question the contributions of Toews or Richards. Denis Savard recently told a story of when he went to Montreal in the Chelios trade.

Serge Savard greeted him and said, "You point production is going to go down, but your going to get your name on the Cup." There is so much more to hockey than point totals. Who's going into the corners, who's going to the net, who is playing defense like Jerry Sloan and Norm Van Lier. (Anyone remember those two mockingly playing defense with their hands behind their back when the ref's called them for a foul!) Who is coming out of the game with bumps, bruises and contusions? Who's taking the body instead of trying to stick check?

Indeed, who is playing like a wild Indian out there? When my brothers, friends and I used to run around the house and yard, expending the boundless energy of youth, on more than one occasion my father exclaimed, "Knock it off. You're acting like a bunch of wild Indians." I know, blasphemy in this day and age of political correctness. Yet in my warped mind, it paints a pretty good description of what the Hawks looked like in period one of Game 5. (On a sad note, I'm sure the Obama administration will be auditing my tax returns now.) A memory of the time us wild Indians put a hole in the ceiling of our basement comes to mind.

My dad, in between trying to provide for his wild tribe, was quite the handy man. He totally remodeled our basement – which turned out to be a double edged sword. You see, after the remodeling was completed, he forbade us to play roller hockey down there anymore. So we didn't – at least when he was home. However, while the cats away the mice will play. I'm not sure why my mom let us get away with it, but we'd push the furniture aside and start banging yo-yo's off the walls. Afterwards, we'd put the furniture back in its place, no worse for the wear. We thought we were a clever bunch.

That was until one day when my brother and I were jousting for the puck and put a hole in the ceiling. As Scooby Doo would say, "Rut row!" For over two years we worried about the ramifications of our disobedience. We all had a good laugh about 2 years later when my dad finally saw the scar in the ceiling. "How did that get there?" he inquired. It's a good thing the Statute of Limitations had expired and he had a cold Schlitz in his hands!

After the time had expired in Game 5, we all let out a collective sigh of relief. Does anyone else besides me feel a little relieved when the # 19, # 81 and # 82 car come out of the pits? If Hossa's back is ok, the result of a vicious cross check to the lower back from Timonen, the puck may never come out of the Flyers zone in Game 6 when this line is on the ice. In my opinion Toews had been saddled with two defensive liabilities in our d-zone. I doubt if you'll hear Patrick Kane's name mentioned in the same sentence with the Frank Selke Trophy in the near future.

Big Buff can also be a little tardy getting back into the D-zone. Helene Elliot a guest writer from the LA Times has written some good, almost unbiased, articles on these playoffs. Her terminology that the Flyers have "skillfully" avoided the slammer made me wonder whose side she was on though! She made an observation in game five on Kopecky that made me chuckle – 'apparently Kopecky's name means "please elbow me in the head," in the Flyer's Slovakian to English dictionary.'

By the way my pick to click is the #81 car. I'm still of the opinion that Hossa is the trump card that will bring the Cup to Chicago and get the monkey off his and our back. Also before drawing this piece to a close, I have to give the people who loudly criticized my favorite Swede, a word of advice; Back Off!

We can only hope the #4 car will be skating with us for some time to come. Many arm chair point men and writers in Chicago laid a yeoman's portion of the blame on Hjarlmarrson for game 4's unfavorable result. To hear the pundits, he did nothing right all night. First off, the face off just prior to the goal, never should have even taken place. The penalty assessed to Kopecky that resulted in the face off, was a routine defensive play for the Flyers that night. Secondly, Niemi should have slammed the door on that one.

Also as Sam Fels pointed out, the # 4 car has been paired with the anti-Sharp, Brent Sopel, quite a bit recently. Sope's seems to be having some problems with the Flyers intense fore-check. My thought – keep Campbell paired with Hjarlmarrson except on the penalty kill. Campbell leads the Hawks defensemen in Corsi ratings by a wide margin. Basically this means Campbell is getting the puck the hell out of our zone.

As Sarah Kustock tried to interview Steegs after game 5, the fans started chanting, "We want the Cup!" Tell me that didn't send some shivers down the old backbone. I'm fairly certain the Hawk players could "feel" the fans passion. So, now that the Hawks know what we want, how do they go about ratcheting up the energy and effort meter another notch? What's it going to take to see our warriors hoist hockey's 35 pound equivalent of the Holy Grail? As usual, I have a thought...

While backpacking in the Flathead Range in Montana many moons ago, we ran into an unforeseen obstacle. We were going to hike over the range and meet Montana Bob's wife, Pat, on the opposite side of the mountains she dropped us off on a few days later. Mind you, it's a five hour ride from point A to point B. As we started our descent back to civilization, we found ourselves in a bit of a quandary. Basically, we kept following false trails that led to dead ends. We even hiked down a dry creek bed for 0.75 miles, with 70# packs, that had boulders that were up to 6 feet tall. That trail ended in a 200 foot waterfall. Despite my friend Tom's solution, "We have rope don't we," we climbed back up the creek bed and tried one more, dead end trail.

Now Montana Bob, who isn't exactly revered for his back country wilderness skills, is one of Montana's premiere "Turdologists." This came in somewhat handy as we saw a huge Bear scat in the middle of our last dead end attempt to descend on the East side of the range. Bob examined the pile of poop, noted it was from a bear and passed along one more bit of information on the fresh pile. He noted that there were pine cones in the bear scat which led him to conclude that the bear, wherever he was lurking, was very, very hungry.

Are you hungry enough to eat pine cones Hawks? Let's devour those Dreamsicles from Philly.

(By the way, I'm almost certain it was my brother John who put the hole in the ceiling!)

Rich Lindbloom

6/11/10

This Cup's for you

Oddly enough, it isn't the irrepressible smiles, bear hugs, boundless joy or awesome photos of the well deserved celebration that occupies my mind. It's a painting by RoseLee Deutsch, the 82 year old "groupy" who has been following the Hawks, the mighty Blackhawks, for almost 6 decades. Through thick and thin she's backed the red clad warriors – and she'll be the first to tell you, "There was a lot of thin!" Gazing upon the painting seems to evoke all those buried feelings of frustration, dashed hope and longing for those who have ventured into the passionate world of Blackhawk hockey.

The painting depicts a broken hearted warrior who wore # 3 for the Hawks, after a crushing defeat in game 7 of the Stanley Cup Finals in 1971. A player who gave his all, only to see his dream, and countless fans, dashed upon the jagged rocks of the fickle finger of fate. As we "skate away – on the thin ice of a new day" as Ian Anderson sings, please know that the evanescent, ebullient joy we are currently experiencing is not Blackhawk hockey. No, Blackhawk hockey is players like Maggie. It's the tears, sweat, sacrifice, bravery and 110% effort. It's the "I've got your back" mentality of the ultimate team sport. The, you mess with him, you mess with me mindset.

When Jonathan Toews accepted the Conn Smythe trophy, I couldn't help but wonder if the right choice had been made. If an individual player was to receive it, my choice would have been Danny Briere. He was a riddle that four very good hockey teams never solved this post season. However, to the victors go the spoils so they say; certainly the #19 car was a worthy choice.

My vote for MVP would have been for a player that goes by the name of "Team." It would not have been only for this hungry group of kids who wore the Indian Head during the 09/10 season. No, I would have included players like Maggie who never left anything but blood, sweat and tears in the arena. Take another look at RoseLee's painting, despite leaving everything he had out on the ice, the portrait screams "I let my team down."

Of course, nothing could be further from the truth.

As I arose so many early mornings the last 8 weeks, the first thing I did was stumble over to the coffee maker. Gazing at Keith's hands in the painting made me contemplate God's incredible design of the human body. My finger tips can sense the difference between the thicknesses of one or two coffee filters – a .002" difference! As this spring ritual of war unfolded, I was constantly reminded of the razor thin margin between victory and defeat.

Think for a moment about all the "ifs" involved in winning the Cup. If not for Kane's and Hossa's miraculous goals against the Preds, or Niemi's face mask save in OT of game three vs. the Sharks we might be singing the blues Chicago is so well known for. If Brian Campbell doesn't risk coming back three weeks earlier than expected or Ladd didn't play with an undisclosed fracture; if Duncan Keith hadn't littered the ice with his choppers or if Bolland had not recovered well enough from the back surgery. (Apparently he studied some of Burr-dogs agitation techniques while recovering.)

In a great team building moment, what if the Hawks had decided not to extend a long road trip by going out of the way to attend Dale Tallon's fathers wake two years ago? Of course I could go on and on. The point is, Stanley Cups are, perhaps more than any other sport, decided by teams, not individuals. Keith Magnuson epitomized that word that has no "I" in it.

Of all the Blackhawk's on this year's squad, Toews probably comes closest to Maggie's desire to win. It's the look of seriousness both players possessed, the insatiable hunger to win. Winning hockey is about a lot of different things; however it is not about personal stats. While the #19 car has not spilled as much blood on the ice as that Blackhawk warrior whose number hangs in the rafters, there is no doubt he would have if necessary. I wonder if Jonathan realizes he's accepting that MVP and Stanley Cup in the name of so many players that slipped the Indian Head over their shoulders during the Hawks storied history.

I'm not sure how the Hawk brass came to the conclusion that a 19 year old would be named team captain, but it proved to be one of the best decisions management ever made. Was it just me or did Toews push his skating up a couple notches in this post season – that cat was fast. Game 6 of the Stanley Cup Finals seem to elevate everyone's play a notch or two. That is, almost everyone…

The Shitzu line seemed to rest a bit after Sunday's explosion. Below is a picture of them in between the 2nd and 3rd periods on Wednesday. They almost single handedly defeated the Flyers in game 5. Flying around the ice seemed to finally take its toll on our normally energetic fur ball line. From left to right, Versteeg, Bolland and Big Buff appeared to be a bit out of gas.

By the way, did you notice that Pronger could not take the puck away from Hossa? The announcer made me laugh when he described Pronger's first penalty. He actually invented a new infraction. After Hossa was cross checked, belted in the head twice and finally held, the announcer said Pronger was sent to the box for "A whole lot of penalty going on there."

Before I go any further, I must take my hat off to the tenacious team from Philadelphia. (Also the Pred's, Canuck's and Sharks.) Sometimes there is no rhyme or reason to who emerges victorious in this battle of attrition. 8th seed my rear end – the Flyers were one very good hockey team. Leino should be made to give a urine sample. Hartnell, who hopefully by now has a shave and hair cut, was a beast. Good luck trying to find enough money to sign Giroux. There is no doubt why Richards wears the "C" on his sweater. He hit Kopecky so hard, momentarily Tomas became Jupiter's 64th confirmed moon.

Some other Flyer tried to duplicate Richard's hit on the # 33 truck. That turned out to be a "big" mistake. You might as well be checking a speeding locomotive. I read Big Buff taunted the peace loving Philly fans by tapping the Plexiglas as he skated by after his goal. What's that old saying, "He who laughs last, laughs best!" Next to Kaner, Buff has the best goal celebration on the team. The key to stopping Buff in my opinion is not getting him ticked off – he appears to have a little Mr. Hyde in him. "Sitting on the Hawks bench, eyeing the Flyers with bad intent," as Jerry McP would put it.

While on the subject of celebrating, the special moment of June 9th, 2010 was shared with my brother John. I received a text from John on Monday morning asking where I'd be watching Game 6. "I'd like to celebrate the championship with you," he stated. If there is such a thing as a buddy system in hockey, my brother John was mine. From the early 70's through 90's we made many a trek up the stairs to the second balcony. We used to park our car on a side street on the South side of the Stadium and pay a kid named Pee-Wee $2 to "watch" it. As the years flew by, Pee-Wee eventually grew to about 6'3". There were many nights we wished the Hawks hustled like that kid watching our car!

Over the course of those years we obviously experienced many highs and lows. The battles with the North Stars were as good as hockey gets. What a moment to see Denis Savard take the ice at the Stadium for the first time. We also saw my favorite Hawk of all time, the #21 car, weave his magic with the Scooter Line. We cheered the Million Dollar Line and cried when the #9 car left for Winnipeg. We were there for that playoff double OT loss to the Sabres, when Gil Perault finally dented that impenetrable fortress known as Tony-O. We cheered the RPM line and watched 51 year old Gordie Howe break rookie Keith Brown's nose with a flying elbow. I know a couple of you sang "Wooly Bully," with us! While he didn't spend a lot of time on the Hawks, I never saw anyone as tough as Bob Probert. Many Sunday nights were spent with our ears glued to the radio as children.

John and I never failed to smile when the organist would play "Three Blind Mice" when the ref and two linesmen would take the ice. Those were the days where there was only one ref and he was usually visually impaired. I can recall driving home listening to the post game show and then Jazz Transfusion on WXRT, hosted by Terry Hemmert. To say that Hawk fans got all Jazzed up after it was finally determined the puck was indeed, "in the mail," would be an understatement. It was such a treat last Wednesday to celebrate the hoisting of the Cup with one of the greatest Hawk fans I know.

And what a game we watched! At one point, after Hossa got penalized for goalie interference, (the worst call in the playoffs in my opinion), I exclaimed, "I can't take this," and stormed to the bathroom. While in the commode, I heard some shouts and was pleasantly surprised to hear Sharpie had struck pay dirt. After that onslaught in the first period, I had hoped we could get a two to three goal lead and coast to the finish line. Instead I felt like Sisyphus rolling that rock up the hill, only to see it tumble back down.

As we hung on for dear life throughout most of the third, the thought of having to watch another game on Friday crossed my mind. So close, yet so far away. When Leino skated through our Neutral Zone **GAP**, I thought game 7, here we come. For the next 8 minutes though, the #31 car came to the rescue like Superman. At least three times I thought the game was over, only to see Niemi somehow keep his net untarnished. As Pat Foley would put it, "Niemi says No!" It's hard to enjoy a hockey game when your sitting in the chair with your arms, fingers and legs crossed. Especially after they kept showing that guy polish the Cup. (How do I apply for that job?) And then it happened...

Not the best, but probably the most dangerous player on the Hawks since Savard found the puck on his stick along the left dashboards. He put a in your face disgrace, chuck and jive, shake and bake, now you see it, now you don't move on the Flyer defenseman and headed towards the net. Kaner fired a shot that was very reminiscent of Crosby's shot in the Olympics from an almost impossible angle. The puck slipped through Leighton's legs, or did it? I'm pretty sure the referee has not signaled goal yet. I heard the obviously in gross denial goal judge refused to turn the goal light on.

The one person who did know it went in started a celebration that will go down in playoff hockey history. I can see that reverse tape of the goal now in the "What if..." series that I enjoyed so much throughout the playoffs. By the time the #88 car had come out of the backstretch, I'm sure Maggie was taking his hands off his head and smiling! M-80's began to explode in the neighborhood. Kaner approached warp speed as he jumped up and flew into Niemi's arms. That is one Hawk who can fly!

The Philly crowd, stunned to the core of their existence, responded with a display of sportsmanship that was reprehensible. A co-worker told me, "Richie, you would have been booing the Flyers if they had won and you were at the U.C." I replied, "Absolutely not." I only despise my opponents while the contest is raging – but never when someone grabs hold of that Cup. I don't care what team you play for. The sight of the Cup being pressed to the sky by a warrior, who has survived roughly 8 weeks of Stanley Cup warfare, has my utmost respect. They'll be plenty of time for loathing next season.

The crowd reaction brought to mind a coaching memory a few years back. In the Homewood In House girl's softball league, I had the good fortune of being paired with Richie Brandt. I'm a bit on the high strung side when it comes to coaching – Richie was as laid back as they come. We were playing one of the more competitive teams in the league one day when we found our selves with only 8 players. I asked the other coach if he could loan me an outfielder and he replied, "Why would I do that?" We then got into a bit of a heated exchange that left this normally mild mannered reporter a bit agitated.

When Richie asked what had happened, he made me laugh with his response to the situation. Rather than get mad at the other coach like I was doing he simply said, "I feel sorry for people that our wound that tight." Philadelphia fans are wound as tight as they come. So once again, I hold out the olive branch to Philadelphia and their fans. In the words of Philadelphia native Todd Rundgren, "Can, we still be friends!"

Well, I suspect most of you kept the midnight lamp burning, soaking in every interview and analysis on the post game show. The best comment I heard was from Steve Konroyd. All season long I've enjoyed and learned from Konroyd's insight into the game. His description of Duncan Keith holding the Cup up was priceless. "Watching the toothless hockey player hoisting the Cup above his head is the quintessential hockey moment." It says it all.

RoseLee did an excellent recap of the unbelievable parade that took place on Friday. In her words;

"Did you get a chance to watch the festivities? A lot of time following busloads of jerseys, but I loved every minute and thought the speakers were great…short and sweet. And do you think that the crowd that stuffed itself into every square inch of the streets and sidewalks satisfied the negative thirst of the complaints about the bandwagon people? All I know is that every new fan that was gained only added to my enjoyment. I loved it when we would leave a game after a win and be swallowed up in the cheering, excited, emotional crowd. I couldn't have cared less who was an old or new fan. And in the shots of the crowd at the celebration today, the numbers of young people made you realize that this is not a sport that is getting left behind."

What a three year ride it has been, worth every speed bump in the road! Blood, sweat, tears, missing teeth and lots of smiles. Troy Murray once noted "That symbol, the Indian warrior, meant more to Maggy than to anyone else I've ever known." Keith Magnuson, it's time for you to raise your battered hands to the sky and let out a war cry"

Number 3 car, this Cup is for you.

By the way, the Lindblooms have a new cat named Stanley. Below is a picture of her and Seabrook eating from the CUP!

CAPOCALYPSE

I first saw the term Capocalypse on the Second City Hockey website. If you were looking for a one word description of the roster decimation of the Stanley Cup Champion Chicago Blackhawks – look no further. It hit home with the crystal clear clarity of a jackhammer. The effects of the Salary cap were a revelation few of us were prepared for.

By the time the dreaded Salary Cap had taken its tormenting toll, the champions were shattered into a thousand bits and pieces. In a sick sort of way it felt like being subjected to one of those high school bullies who twist your arm behind your back until you scream, "Uncle!" When the dust had finally settled, 10 very popular Hawks found new ponds to skate on next year.

The decimation of our roster seems to bring a new insight into Juliet's reluctant goodnight to Romeo when she so wistfully laments "parting is such sweet sorrow." While I wouldn't go so far as to compare Juliet waxing poetically about Romeo leaving her that evening, the loss of Versteeg, Byfuglien, Barker, Burrish, Ladd, Madden, Niemi, Eager, Fraser and Sopel has left many Hawk fans downtrodden and brokenhearted.

All ten of those players have left us with many fond remembrances in the 09/10 season. While some player's contributions were more noticeable than others, they all were pieces in the puzzle that eventually resulted in the hoisting of the Cup. Actually, winning the Cup was every bit as hard as trying to assemble a blue sky in a 10,000 piece puzzle. Both require an inordinate amount of persistence and a lot of trial and error. I know I'm not the only one who has tried to force a puzzle piece into place.

There's a great book entitled *Kitchen Table Wisdom* by Rachel Naomi Remen that I would highly recommend. In one of the chapters she describes a puzzling table her father would leave set up in their living room. The pieces of the puzzle would be emptied out with only one stipulation; the cover of the box that showed the picture you were supposed assemble was sequestered away. As family and friends would gather together, they would occasionally take a stab at putting together a few of the pieces (painstakingly in my impatient, non-puzzling mind!). Eventually, the puzzle would begin to take shape.

As a doctor, obviously she was using the puzzle as an analogy of life. We're really never quite sure what the next piece is, are we? Leave it to me to see the parallels between a puzzle and the Blackhawks. (Whoever said men have a one track mind was probably on to something.) Robert Frost said he could sum up in three words what he knew about life; *"It goes on."* As much as we'd like to linger, savoring every precious moment of last season, it's time to dump a new puzzle out on the table as we attempt to defend our title. "Defend our title," has such a nice ring to it, although I'm sure most of the naysayers have already written us off; big mistake.

I think one thing the new Hawk fans have to realize, is that the bloody attrition that resulted from the Salary Cap catastrophe was not an attempt by team management to reduce payroll. Signing Hossa, Campbell, Toews, Kane, Keith and severely limited our options. Is anybody particularly fond of losing one of those stallions? How many teams in the league would bury Huet's $5.6 million dollar contract in Switzerland? (On a side note, how many of you remember Switzerland defeated us last year!)

Prior to the 2004 strike, it was reported 2/3rds of the NHL clubs were losing money. It's hard to get fans to come out to support a team when they're 20 games below .500. As RoseLee insightfully noted *"The salary cap was not designed to make all of us happy."* No, in my mind it was designed to create parity in the league which ultimately should increase the fan base and excitement. While not "all good" it's certainly not all bad.

A team that finished out of the playoffs last year has a legitimate chance to be playing for the Cup the next season. Making the playoffs has a tendency to jump start any struggling franchise. Contrary to uninformed opinion, not everyone makes the playoffs in hockey; only 16 out of 30 teams advance into post season battles. Actually, the last two weeks of the regular season can start to resemble playoff hockey as teams on the cusp battle for the 8th and final spot.

If the truth be known, I'm somewhat excited to see to see how the puzzle pieces will fit together this year. Ever the optimist, RoseLee noted that *"if a couple of these new additions live up to expectations, we might start to see a lot of new names on the red shirts around town."* While I doubt we'll see many jerseys with the names Lalonde, Brophey,

Bickell, Beach, Skille, Crawford or Leddy this fall – clearly their time to shine has come. (Actually, there may be a few damsels with a Stahlberg jersey on before long - truly, just "a hunk, a hunk of burning hockey player.")

Of course the pieces they'll attempt to replace will not turn out to be a stroll in the park. How can you replace the Versteegian Rhapsody? Who will the new psychoanalysts be now that Dr. Burrish and his associate Ben Eager are gone? (I wonder how much they charged for their session with Burrows.) Our goalies will have to make 3 or more saves a game now that the human shot blocker, Brent Sopel, is history. With Laddie gone, who's going to pound Kesler for us? Who is going to be Barking like a dog on our blue line?

The steadying influence and bulging bicep of Madden will most certainly be missed. It will be interesting to see how Fraser, and his "tall don't scare me attitude," does in Edmonton. I always appreciated what the #46 car brought to the ice. Dustin Byfuglien, hockey's version of baseball's Mr. October, Reggie Jackson, will be somewhat irreplaceable. 260 pound thumpers are hard to come by. Do you think the Hawk organization might show a replay of Dustin's obliteration of Pronger on the Jumbo-Tron a few times this year? That evil villain flying into the boards is an image that's indelibly etched upon my mind.

While most of you are probably too young to remember The Lone Ranger, there was a saying at the end of every show that would be a good way to describe the time Antti Niemi spent with the Hawks. There would be no more terrorists in the world if the Lone Ranger and Tonto could still get on a horse. Hell, they could ride at a full gallop, picking off bad guys like a bug zapper on a hot summer's night. Of course it helped that their six-shooters never ran out of bullets. After the bad guys were apprehended, The Lone Ranger would head off into the sunset – always followed by the query "Who was that masked man, anyway?"

From his first game in Finland this year, until his stubborn refusal to let the Flyers tickle his twine in overtime of game 6, the #31 car was a key piece to the puzzle. I realize, like that old Winston cigarette commercial, that it's what's up front that counts. Certainly Niemi had some talented teammates in front of him. Yet there is absolutely no

145

doubt his stellar play throughout the playoffs had a huge part in the Hawks inscribing their names on Lord Stanley's Cup. Anyone who tries to diminish what he did in the nets for us by saying he had great players in front of him needs to have their head examined and then be drawn and quartered.

Actually Antti played quite a few more games than another goalie for the Hawks who played briefly in 1938. There's a good chance that no NHL goalie ever played less in a season than Alfie Moore and still had their name inscribed on the Cup. The exploits of Alfie Moore are chronicled in Brian McFarlane's great book, *Best of the Original Six*. What a great and highly informative read.

I'll give you the truncated version but I highly recommend you pick that book up. Suffice it to say Alfie, who was hoping to scrounge up a ticket for the Stanley Cup opener, was literally dragged out of a bar in mid afternoon and standing between the pipes for the Hawks that evening. Reportedly, the Hawks coach, Bill Stewart got into a fist fight with Conn Smythe, the Leafs owner, before the game. (I'm thinking he smelled a little alcohol on Alfie's breath.)The Hawks starting goalie could not get his foot in his boot do to a broken toe suffered in the semi finals. Moore was the only goalie that Smythe would let play in his place. "...that is if you can find him," Smythe snidely remarked. Apparently Smythe knew Alfie had a little Mr. Bo Jangles in him.

On the first Leaf shot of the game, they got one past the rapidly sobering net minder. However, he blanked the Leafs the rest of the game and the Hawks won the opener 3-1. As he skated off the ice, Alfie thumbed his nose at Conn Smythe. As a result Smythe refused to let Alfie tend the nets in any more games!

The Hawks lost the second game when a minor leaguer filled in, but somehow Mike Karakas managed to jam his swollen foot in his skate for games 3 and 4. After a 4-1 victory in game 4, the Cinderella Hawks had won their second Stanley Cup – a Cup by the way that contains the name of the surprise starter in Game One, Alfie Moore.

While Antti played a bit more than one game for us this year, he certainly is bound to become a footnote in Blackhawk folklore. The unfortunate part is, it appears he signed with the Sharks for what the Hawks would have given him. David Haugh of the Tribune must have read the book, *The 7 Habits of highly Successful Hockey Players.* He nailed it when he said the Niemi negotiations turned out to be a Lose/Lose proposition for everyone involved. In an interview he asked Niemi if it was true the Hawks offered him $8 million for 3 years – a question Antti declined to answer. As a result of the failed negotiations, decades from now Hawk fans may find themselves asking, "Who was that masked man between the pipes, anyway?"

As the truncated ten rode off into the sunset, I began to ponder some of the some of the other the other disasters in the Hawk's roster reconfigurations. As Jane Ace noted "time wounds all heals," and try as I may, it's hard to recall the devastating effect of hearing that The Golden Jet was leaving for Winnipeg. As is the case with all major disasters, it seems the irrepressible will of the human spirit forges on. (How else can you explain Wrigley Field being sold out year after year?) As the Godfather of Soul would put it, "It is what it is." We have no choice at this point but to "take it to the bridge."

Obviously, we are entering unchartered territories as we cross that harrowing, seemingly bottomless ravine of the Salary Cap. Given the choice, we'd all like to see last year's team remain intact. The increasingly nauseating catch phrase, "It's all good," certainly appears to have met its match as we painstakingly watched the Hawks dismembered this past summer. It was a bit like watching Jack Bauer interrogate a terrorist. Clearly, not all was good.

However, we still have 4 of the top 25 players in the league. Think back a moment and tell me when we could last make that statement. We may just hear Chelsea Dagger a few more times than we're anticipating! If things really go bad, maybe we could go with two lines in the third period this year. Take heart Hawkheads, certainly new heroes will emerge, as well as new objects of our arm chair derision. When one considers the puzzle analogy, it's obvious we already have the border in place.

As we head into the season, I can't help but hearing the "Lions and Tigers and Bears, oh my," refrain. (Or is it Canucks and Sharks and Wings, oh my...) It's a foreboding forest were entering. On the positive side of the ledger, we should be treated to a very exciting pre-season. We'll have to be patient with this team as the puzzle begins to take shape. I'm hoping by December some of the pieces will have fallen into place. As Emily Dickinson noted;

'Hope is the thing with feathers
That perches in the soul –
And sings the tune without words
And never stops – at all.

However, if things do head South this season, if Capocalypse does turn out to be our worst nightmare – well may be we can get Sam to entertain us with a few jokes in the upper reaches of section 320 in between periods. As they say, "Laughter is the best medicine," although dancing may come in a close second.

In closing, (yes, finally), the effects of Capocalypse remind me of a great old movie "Zorba the Greek." At the end of the movie a contraption that was devised to haul lumber from the hills to the sea is given a test run. By the time the third log is sent hurtling down, everything collapses like a row of dominoes. All that sweat, hard work and effort result in nothing but the abject futility of man's endeavors. After all their dreams are dashed, the Englishman who was somewhat mesmerized by Zorba's outlook on life, asks him to teach him how to dance. I don't know if this will work for us, but it was a perfect ending to the movie.

Take it from someone who could throw it down with the best of them, James Brown; "It is what it is." It just might resemble "The Funky Chicken" for awhile. It would appear Coach Q is going to have to spend some time at the puzzling table. It's pretty clear that, "papa's got a brand new bag."